Issues of the Soul

THE CORE AND ETHIC OF SOME OF THE MOST IMPORTANT ASPECTS OF LIFE AND DEATH

Issues of the Soul

THE CORE AND ETHIC OF SOME OF THE MOST IMPORTANT ASPECTS OF LIFE AND DEATH

Richard H. Cox

RESOURCE *Publications* · Eugene, Oregon

Resource Publications
A division of Wipf and Stock Publishers
199 W 8th Ave, Suite 3
Eugene, OR 97401

Issues of the Soul
The Core and Ethic of Some of the Most
Important Aspects of Life and Death
By Cox, Richard H., MD, PhD

ISBN 13: 978-1-60899-567-7
Publication date 4/14/2010
Previously published by InSync Press, 2001

Table of Contents

Preface

Many years of study in the fields of psychology, theology, and medicine and over fifty years of professional practice have taught me that everything in life has substance; however, we usually only see the trappings of that substance — the things around substance — not the substance itself. The substance itself I call "ethic." Every part of life, that is, each slice, must be looked at in depth to appreciate it. Like a pie, it must be cut open and eaten to be fully appreciated. The very substance of the pie cannot be understood except bite by bite. Although life has a special beauty when viewed as a whole, its intrinsic beauty is only known when it is sliced and eaten. Each topic discussed in this book is only a small slice of one's life. However, in my experience, they are slices that when attended to fully make for a richer, fuller life.

Substance — ethic — is the stuff life is made of, not the spin-off, not the results, or the side effects. The real thing — the ethic — often eludes us. Perhaps that is because in our earth-bound human state we see only "through a glass darkly," or maybe it is because to see essence in bits and pieces is more comfortable and less threatening. If we could see life in its entirety, the whole of life with its parts and pieces, it would be overwhelming.

By the time we are old enough to even barely perceive what life is really made of, most of it has already happened and cannot be changed. However, since we are part of it, and will pass it on in everything from our attitudes to our genes, it is important that we attempt to understand it and, as the famous prayer goes, "change the things we can, and accept the things we cannot."

If the musings and anecdotes in this book help to open even one squinted eye to the real meaning of even one slice of life, including the author's, it will have accomplished its purpose.

About the Author

Dr. Richard H. Cox is President Emeritus/Professor of the Forest Institute, a graduate school of professional psychology and an intergen-erational living community in Springfield, Missouri. He holds earned doctorates in psychology, medicine, and theology and has been awarded two honorary doctorates. He is the author of numerous professional and popular articles, as well as author and co-author of several professional books. Dr. Cox is recognized nationally and internationally as a conference speaker, consultant, and for his work in human services involving medicine, psychology, and theology. He is also a professional musician. He has worked in the field of professional human services for over fifty years.

Introduction

The first few words of this book could cause one to believe that it might be philosophical. It is not. It is an attempt to carefully slice out some of the pieces of the whole of life and look at them in depth, yet informally. Distinction is made among the words *ethos, ethic,* and *ethics* to help the reader understand the context in which a number of real-life categories are discussed in a serious yet light, anecdotal, and autobiographical fashion. The words *ethos, ethic,* and *ethics* are all derived from a common source, the Greek word *ethikos. Ethos* is the fundamental character or spirit of a person, a society, or culture. It is the foundation material of a person, a society, or a group. Ethos characterizes and distinguishes the behavior of that individual or group. It is the substance, the matrix, the *ethereal* (ethe + real), and the *real.* Like ether, another derivative of the same Greek word, ethos is an imaginative, tenuous, poetic part of speech that has its root in that light, airy gas that can put one to sleep. However, there is nothing unreal about ethos. It simply invites us to look at the real and seemingly unreal presentation of it. Ethos is the cell and its membrane, but not the function of the cell.

At times the behavior of any given individual or group appears to be a combination of the real and the unreal. Actually, however, this appearance is due to the fact that some aspects of behavior emanate from within and other aspects are externally superimposed by the regulations (ethics) of the group or by society. It is often difficult for individuals or groups to distinguish even within themselves those beliefs and behaviors that are intrinsically driven and those that are extrinsically demanded. ***Ethos*** becomes that accumulated, carefully organized yet disorganized, uncontrolled but regulated, sociological part of a culture that gives a corporate image or specific identity to a given subculture. It is the underlying substance that provides the fuel for beliefs, customs, and practices.

Practices and customs of a given community are called folkways and mores. These practices are accepted without conscious assent or choice, but nonetheless serve to control the life of those living within that community. The mores and folkways of a society do not determine ethos; ethos determines the mores and folkways. Mores and folkways are the intrinsic elements that are controlled by the extrinsic elements that are controlled by the intrinsic nature of any society. This process is a circular one in which the inside controls the outside and in return the outside controls the inside. Folkways and mores are extremely difficult to change due to this fact. The mores and folkways constitute the fabric of a given society. When fabric is made, thread is woven in both directions, forming a pattern that is intrinsic and constitutes such a part of the material that it cannot be removed. This weaving process of warp and woof is a dynamic illustration of how the slices of genetics, education, and experience are woven together into the fabric of life. There is, however, a distinct difference in the analogy of the warp and woof of a fabric and the mores and folkways of a society. The difference is that once the fabric is woven, it does not change except to wear and eventually disintegrate. The mores and folkways of society are forever changing, and instead of disintegrating, they continue to form the very matrix of society. In most instances, mores and folkways change so slowly that they are not noticed. The twentieth century, particularly the latter half of it, may be an exception to this observation. The value-base structure of the Western world society is certainly appreciably different from that which ordered the earlier half of the century. On the other hand, from the turn of the nineteenth century to the middle of the twentieth century there were also major changes. It may well be that the slow, insidious process of change in social thought eclipses our ability to see it except in retrospect.

Ethic differs from ethos in that it is that body of moral principles derived from ethos. Each slice of life has its own unique *ethic.* Whereas ethos is virtually impossible to change, ethic can be changed. Ethic contains a conscious element. Ethic contains our assent. Ethic contains our willingness to cooperate. Ethic contains our permission. Ethic contains our choice. Ethic, by definition, is what we do with ethos. It is what we do with the very substance that is us. Ethic is not that code which we call ethics. Ethic, however, is the stuff we take from ethos and extrapolate into that code of ethics. Ethic becomes the distinctive substance by which a group or culture governs itself. Although this ethic is invariably translated into what we call "ethics," it is much deeper, much more alive, and much more intangible. It is the "esprit de corps" which never gets translated in a literal fashion. In fact, it is so indigenous that translation is not possible.

Although individuals within a group may differ in their individual *ethics,* the body-ethic remains the same. Regardless of individualized and personal *ethic,* the corporate, societal, and group *ethic* remains uniform. Professional bodies and organizations have codes of *ethics,* which frequently seem to be quite contrary to the articulated *ethic* of the particular group. In other words, what the organization should look like may not even closely resemble what its individual members look like. Today's practice within the healing professions offers a splendid example of a profession that proclaims its *ethic* as being warm, caring, and as abiding by the Hippocratic oath, which promises to "do no harm." Yet, some persons in the United States would question whether the profession as a whole practices *ethics* in accord with its *ethic.* The "ethos" and "ethics" of most physicians I know would embody the deepest desire to help in a way that today's "managed care" will not allow. Further, the individual "ethics" of most physicians drive them to attempt to treat their patients in a caring fashion. However, the current "ethic" of the profession prohibits both the ethos and the ethics from succeeding. This is a perfect example to show that while *ethos* is beyond our control, the body-*ethic* can and does change, but often produces incongruent *ethics.*

Ethics differs from both ethos and ethic. This term represents the combined elements from ethos, out of which one unconsciously chooses (or has thrust upon one) how to live one's daily life, and differs from ethic by dealing with the minutia, which if not dealt with in the accepted *ethical* way often become problems of great magnitude. The difference between ethic (singular) and ethics (plural) is not just grammatical. It is a matter of body identity (ethic) and the way that body attempts to regulate its members' behavior (ethics).

The *ethics* of a profession or group are expected behaviors of the members of that profession or group, usually set forth in written form, but are determined largely by a few within it. The members must then accept those ethical "principles" and agree to abide by them. When they do not, the group or profession sanctions and disciplines them for not doing so. Since the group or profession espouses a rigid "ethical standard," it portrays an external image of being highly moral. The discrepancy between the "code of ethics" and the behavior of those within the group or profession is frequently gigantic. Further, the "ethics" of a profession or group frequently actually prevent persons within that group from carrying out the basic "ethos" of it.

I have chosen to use the word *ethic* (Greek *ethikos*) in discussing the slices of life in this book because it is the core, the essences, and the substantive gestalt that give definition to various aspects of human existence. Ethic is not *what* we do. It is what *causes* us to do what we do. If we are to have any understanding of life itself, we must take it a slice at a time and taste it very carefully.

I once visited a factory where foods were produced. An entire staff of persons painstakingly tasted the products. Each "taster" would take a small morsel, smell it, look at it, and then in a most exquisite way taste it. They were trained to know what it should look like, smell like, and taste like. They were able to distinguish between the subtleties of aromas and tastes. Only with that careful analysis could they produce a product that as a whole had value. So it is with the slices of life. A full appreciation of each aspect of our life requires that we be willing to cut each slice into smaller slices and "smell," "observe," and "taste" each part critically and then put each slice back into the whole "pie of life" in an integrated way. Just as some slices in the food plant were discarded, we must be willing to do the same — to go back to the "drawing board" and start over.

In the study of the human body, we know that there are powerful hormones, but in back of them are substances called "releasing factors," and in back of the releasing factors are signals that stimulate those factors. Likewise, ethic (that core of the person) is the unseen but real, immeasurable but most obvious, silent but very much heard part of human existence that makes us what and who we are. Ethic as a concept, a definition, and a descriptor of various areas of the human struggle is the core of the discussion in this book.

While "ethos" is too big and "ethics" too bureaucratically dictated, "ethic" is within our grasp to change. While "ethics" is the part we see and "ethos" the part to which we ascribe, "ethic" is really what we are. Furthermore, our "ethic" will, and does, invariably change, whether or not we attempt to change it or even wish that it would change. We do have the ability as human beings with frontal lobes in the brain to "make up our minds" and thus change the nature of our life experiences and, perhaps, even modify our inner selves.

The chapters in this book are my thoughts on a few topics, punctuated with reflections and experiences from my own life. Each reader will hopefully replace the anecdotes with his or her own and therefore find new energy in integrating the present with individual histories and futures.

1

Culture and Society

The culture ethic is a mirror of the human soul and the collective image of society.

There are two kinds of culture: adaptive and genetic. *Adaptive* culture is that which evolves both in the development of society and as a result of societal demands. Some of those demands are known, but most are not. In many ways, adaptive culture is both the driver and the driven. That which is doing the driving is so inextricably interwoven with that which results from the driving that it cannot be separated. In many ways, it like the age-old "chicken and egg" question. It is differentiated from *genetic* culture in that it is fluid. Further, it is more observable. Most importantly, adaptive culture is not measurable by any known scientific formula or instrument. Society is the mirror of culture, not the other way around. Many would have us believe that culture is derived from societal evolution. Not so. Culture is the deeply rooted foundation upon which society is built and the rationale for behaving as we do.

Genetic culture is located deep within the recesses of societal structure. In fact, it is so deep that we mistake societal structure for culture. Genetic culture changes slowly and is not absolutely static. However, whereas adaptive culture may show change within a generation, genetic culture may require many generations to show change. It may be seen as developing out of generations of values, beliefs, prejudices, and practices. It may even be viewed through the eyes of Carl Jung, the Swiss psychoanalyst who postulated the theory of the "collective unconscious." It was his belief that the collective unconscious is inherited and upon it is built the whole structure of personality. He did not go so far as to propose that it is biological; however, there is no doubt that he believed it to be just as real. I would agree with that belief. The inborn conscious and unconscious personality structures, out of which arise the foundations of society, are patently obvious to even the most casual observer. Genetic culture, as differentiated from adaptive culture, is measurable by anthropological and social science professionals. Although it is not politically popular to talk about ethnic, racial, and individual differences, they are present, observable, and measurable.

Benjamin Franklin wrote a lengthy list of *Rules of Civility* in an attempt to influence the adaptive culture. They have to do with behavior in public, respect for others' property and person, human decency, and dignity. Of course, these rules did not work in Mr. Franklin's day and they do not work now. However, in the professional graduate school setting in which I currently work, Franklin's rules are proudly posted under glass (slightly modified to fit our profession) for everyone to see. The hope is that students, faculty, staff, and patients will at least glance at this framed treasure and perhaps momentarily reflect on a bit more civility. Sometimes that seems to happen.

Most of us cannot do a whole lot about the genetic aspects of culture. Of course, as time goes on, human genetic changes are inevitably being produced, whether we wish it to happen or not, by the food we eat, the air we breathe, the water we drink, and our choices of reproductive mates, as well as by natural processes. As cloning progresses, and until it becomes a regular practice, which it almost certainly will, genetic culture will be in the hands of the scientists. But it will not stay that way. In the beginning, cattle breeding for genetic purposes was in the hands of the scientists in animal husbandry, just as cloning is in the hands of many of those same scientists today. However, every cattle entrepreneur is now in the process of "upgrading" the herd by making genetic choices in the breeding process. Non-degreed and scientifically untrained farmers are now able to make profound changes in the herd culture. Inevitably, cloning will go the same way. Scientists, societies, and even families will be able to "upgrade" not only their cattle but also the family and society "stock."

It all seems complicated now to most of us, just as selective breeding seemed complicated many years ago. When cloning becomes better understood and more commonplace, it too will become much less controlled by the scientists and be placed in the public domain. Dr. Steven Hawking, the renowned scientist from Cambridge, stated in an address at the White House that "...the combination of advanced science and technology will inevitably bring together incredible changes — including genetically engineered human beings...unless we have a totalitarian world order, someone will design an improved human somewhere..." (*Newsleader,* March 7, 1998).

Human engineers are now capable of changing the pattern of family heredity by selective "outbreeding" of fetuses that in their opinion are not capable of human life as defined by the "experts." An embryo can be engineered to be born with the color of eyes and hair, kind of complexion, and even the gender of a parent's choice. There is little room for doubt that soon we will choose to selectively breed persons with certain types of personalities as well. This new method of reproductive control, like the control of anything, will have two sides. While ethical scientists may see it as a method for bettering the human race, others may see it as a method for less than altruistic ends. Although we decry "ethnic cleansing" and although genetic manipulation is doubtless seen as more humane, it nonetheless could become simply another kind of "ethnic cleansing." The "scientists" who would make such decisions would see them as being for the betterment of the human race, but what is to say that Frankenstein would not have his day and finally find a place in real life?

Culture as the core of ourselves, the "ethic," reflects our philosophy about ourselves. We insert into our spoken philosophy our attitudes about those of our race who have gone before us and those who are yet to be born. However, we are not really too concerned about either those who are no longer here or those who are yet to be here. We are most concerned with ourselves who are here and the effect the others who are here will have on us. Selective genetics says nothing about the unborn. The unborn are not our concern. Our concern is with ourselves, not those not yet born. It is with how we handle the unborn, should they be born. It is with how we deal with them before they are born and how we determine whether or not they should be permitted to be born. We are concerned particularly with those who make life more difficult for us, the born and the unborn. Sometimes we wax gracious and discuss the unborn who may be deemed incapable of enduring our definition of survival; in that case, to prevent them from being born is a generous gesture made on their behalf. It makes us sound humane and generous to spare those who may be born "handicapped" the perils of surviving in our world. At the farthest end of the "handicapped" spectrum this may be easier to understand. The problem is not in the understanding but in the power to set the dividing line between those who should and should not be born and those who should and should not be allowed to live. We see those who are so tragically crippled that it would appear they could only "take" from us, yet they often make incredible contributions. Think of Helen Keller, Ray Charles, Steven Hawking, and a multitude of other outstanding persons who would have proven so many of our theories wrong. In truth, many persons with severe limitations often outstrip others who seemingly have few, if any, limitations.

The same dilemma is true of the impossible choices now having to be made in regard to organ transplants. Who is to say that the twenty-five-year-old will have more to "offer," and thus receive the transplant, than the sixty-five-year-old? The culture ethic is the mirror of the human soul and the collective image of society.

Technological developments change our ethic. They force us to face all over again the questions we thought we had answered. As our existence takes on more and more artificial intelligence, as well as the answers that come from that kind of intelligence, we will be forced into more and more linear and calculated thinking, rather than thinking that leaves room for individual differences. No doubt the most revolutionary development in the past several generations has been the computer. It may very well be as important as the discovery of fire. Everything changed. So it is with the computer. The computer is not simply another machine, like the sewing machine or automobile. It not only changes the *way* we do things; it changes *what* we do. It not only makes thinking easier; it changes what we think. As a result, our core — ethic — is in one of the most dramatic and traumatic revolutions in the history of the human race.

Let us consider what culture is not. Its purpose is not to demonstrate what we know. Knowledge has little to do with culture. If culture were to do with knowledge, culture as an ethic of the people would at best be mediocre, representing the average IQ of the human race, which is by test measurement 90 to 110. Culture is about ethic. It is not about etiquette, manners, or even behavior. The purpose of culture is not to show who we are or even who we hope to become. The culture ethic reveals whom we respect and why. Although these two issues may seem very much alike, they are not. In the first instance, culture is for our own ego magnification and exhibition; in the second instance, culture is the result of the combination of adaptive and genetic forces.

Culture therefore becomes the soul of society revealed in total nudity, with every mole, wart, and zit on public display. It demands that we show reverence for life, reverence for the living, and reverence for the dead. It subsumes those factors and influences that made us who we are and includes those factors that will endure in subsequent generations after we are gone.

There is a tremendous amount of discussion in the United States about "equal rights," "equal opportunity," "ethnic prejudice," and other issues that are issues only because our culture has defined them as such. Without the knowledge of cultural expectation, many "prejudices" would not develop in the first place, and those that did develop would not be prejudices but individual opinions. They are "prejudices" because culture has chosen to define them as such. Many other inequalities of human life are found in human relationships, but because they have not been defined as "prejudices," they are considered idiosyncrasies or individual differences.

Further, we attempt to change these undesirable aspects of life by attacking them issue by issue. But it has not worked and is not working. Gordon Allport and numerous other social psychologists have repeatedly pointed out that culture is not changed from the outside in. External forces may change adaptive behavior, but the culture remains the same. Today, when certain ethnic slurs are not acceptable in public, we all know that in private people refer to ethnic groups in the same way they have from the beginning of time. The Old

Testament is rife with ethnic inequality and prejudice, as is the New Testament, classical literature, modern literature, and everything in between.

I had the marvelous privilege as a child of being exposed to a wide variety of life-styles, ethnicities, and religions. Growing up in the poorer areas of a small Midwestern city, I was not shielded from reality by even middle-class standards. As a child, my neighborhood consisted of the married, divorced, common-law, and doubtless a variety of other arrangements of which I was unaware. Among the latter were "two old maids" who had lived together for years and probably had a way of life that the seniors in our neighborhood surely knew, but that I did not.

There were enough ethnic groups that my vocabulary was rich with words that I cannot use in print and would not use today. Our houses were close enough together that we could hear the neighbors' arguments and, regardless of our "prejudices," what people called each other even within their own households. I knew the "proper" names for those ethnic folk and was truly surprised when I learned that other names existed that were considered more respectful. I knew that I was "poor white trash" and wasn't too bothered by it. Why should I have been? It was true. Who else would be grateful for a Thanksgiving basket full of food from unknown donors and unlabeled cans of food from the "relief depot." I can remember my mother crying when she opened two unlabeled cans of peaches and had to say, "This will have to be supper, we can't open any more." Why canned food handed out by government subsidy was unlabeled I do not know to this day.

It wasn't that my father did not work, for he surely did, two or more jobs at a time. There just wasn't enough work or pay in those depression-era days. Even with multiple jobs, the less fortunate could not keep the rent paid and food on the table. My father died on the Fourth of July. It only seems appropriate that he was relieved of his eighty-seven-year-old work-worn physical temple on Independence Day, 1985.

Material things certainly were welcome, but somehow what people thought about you was more important than the physical things you had. Maybe that was because we all had (or didn't have) about the same amount of very little. A person's color or nationality didn't seem to matter. Some of the folks who cared the most about "us kids" didn't go to our church, didn't speak English without an accent, and weren't of the same color. We didn't seem to notice any of that. The richness of that kind of "poverty" cannot be measured.

I remember the little "old" lady who ran a small store around the corner. I suspect that in truth she was not "old" at all, except in my childhood perception. She never asked how many pennies we had; she just filled a sack with all kinds of candies and took whatever number of coins we gave her. Cookies were displayed in large cardboard boxes and sold in the "bulk," a method that would surely cause a public health officer to shudder today. She had marshmallow cookies covered with chocolate, wafer cookies that we called "ice-cream cookies," and "windmill" cookies that we liked to dunk in milk. The overhead fan and cellophane paper kept the flies off of them, for the most part. She went out of business by the time I was about eight or nine — maybe her generosity was part of the reason. I do know that she looked forward to "us kids" coming into her store. As I look back on those experiences, it is clear that she gave us more than candy and we gave her more than pennies.

However, we did not see ourselves as experiencing poverty. "Poorness," yes; poverty, no. Poverty was not having a house to live in — we had a house. Poverty was not having a job at all — Dad had several. Poverty was being hungry and not even having unlabeled canned goods. It was understood that being poor had nothing to do with honesty or ambition. Just because you didn't have something did not mean that you could cheat or steal to get it. There was no assumption that "poorness" or even abject poverty produced crime. We had no doubt that crime could produce poverty, but not the other way around.

That belief was correct. The assumption in today's socialistic thinking that poverty produces crime is patently incorrect and furthers both poverty and crime. To work when one could get work was honest. To work to find work was honest. To be poor even when one worked was honest. To be dishonest either when working or not working was a crime. The crime was in not working or not attempting to find work! When we blame the ills of our society upon lack of employment, we give permission to be dishonest rather than industrious. When we allow ourselves to think that poverty produces crime, we give permission for those who have not to steal from those who have. When we claim that poverty produces dishonesty, we subrogate the goodness of the human soul to a social definition of good. History is replete with illustrations from the rich and poor alike who would not sacrifice their internal goodness for external demands, even to the point of willing to face death rather than accept dishonesty.

True poverty is poverty of the spirit. True poverty of the spirit begets physical and material poverty. No one would doubt that to be destitute affects the spirit and produces even more poverty of the soul; however, it is important that we see the cyclical nature of poverty rather than only see it as a one-way street, that is, from poverty to crime. Poverty of spirit robs us of the energy of the soul to move against the odds, to go against the tide, and gives in to depression of more than a psychological sort. When the spirit of life is no longer in the salmon, it cannot swim upstream. When the spirit of life is no longer in the human, it succumbs to illness and death. However, to argue that when the spirit of life is no longer there the human turns to crime is to say that it takes less energy to steal, lie, cheat, kill, or plunder than it does to climb out of the pit. Thousands of success stories tell us that such is not the case.

Further, we give excuse to those who are poverty stricken to turn to drugs. Although poverty does not turn one to drugs, there is certainly no doubt that drugs can turn one to poverty. And there is no doubt that drugs can turn one to crime. This fact has been proven by the rich and poor alike.

The argument is not with the results of poverty, drugs, or crime. The argument is with the causes. Like so many things in our society, we look for the blame, not the cause. The logic breaks down very quickly when we ask the simple question, "If there were no poverty, would there be crime?" The answer is obviously yes. If we then ask the question, "If there were no crime, would there be poverty?" the answer is obviously also yes. There has always been both poverty and crime. The issue is not whether both would exist. The issue is one of blame and cause. It is more than evident that if we must blame, which is a useless thing to do, more poverty comes from crime than crime comes from poverty. Further, to argue *because* one is poor that it gives *reason* to commit crime is simply an illogical excuse.

Our society has made victims of many who could have become conquerors. We have robbed them of their ability and the reward for winning by presuming that crime is a result of, rather than a cause of, poverty.

The same is true of "prejudice." Our society looks for "reasons" for human behavior rather than "causes." When things go wrong, we look to place blame. We do not look to find the cause. Just like poverty and crime, there has always been prejudice. It was there in the first family of the Old Testament. They had two sons. The father loved one more than the other, and one brother hated the other. It is here today. It will be here tomorrow. We spend so much of our energy on attempting to get rid of prejudice, but we would be better off spending that time and money on dealing with the causes.

Psychological knowledge assures us that rarely is the prejudice directly linked to that which is obvious. Instead, due to a mental mechanism called "displacement," we kick something only remotely related to that with which we are upset. The old story of the person who gets upset at work and goes home and kicks the cat is true. The feelings, the cat, and the action are not related — they are only in our life space and available at the same time.

Racial and ethnic prejudice was a new experience for me when I went away to college. I knew that "colored people" went to "their own church," but I thought it was because they wanted to and surely had nothing to do with their being unwelcome at other places. I ate in their homes and they ate in ours. I wasn't aware that there were restaurants or other places in which they were not welcome.

Since we lived on the railroad tracks, our porch posts nearly always had chalk marks on them. This was the way that "bums" told their fellow travelers that a certain house was a good place to get a handout. The handout usually was given in exchange for at least some menial work — bringing in some firewood or a few buckets of coal or maybe helping in the vegetable garden. These folks traveled together by hitching rides on the freight trains and were of all ethnic groups; maybe they were the counterpart of our homeless today in those depression years. We had precious little, but I don't recall us ever turning anyone away. The unspoken feeling was "there but for the grace of God go I." It was not uncommon to hear of someone from the community who left all the sudden, and it was rumored that they had "hit the rails." Sometimes these folks (they were all men, that I knew about) would return months later when more work became available.

There were many Jews in our town. I worked in their stores selling shoes, clothes, and furniture. They were good to me and to many of my schoolmates who needed work. My uncle, William Rozitsky, was a Jew, a wonderful human being. Uncle Billy, so the story goes, married my Irish aunt, was immediately thrown out of the synagogue for marrying a gentile, and had to be buried outside the Jewish cemetery. He often went to our church, and he attended our Protestant wedding. I learned many Hasidic tales and much about Judaism from him. He loved ice cream, and so do I — maybe that's why.

"Prejudice" became real to me when I was pastor of a small church in a Midwestern city. We chose to have the choir from a black congregation sing in our all-white church and to share in a potluck dinner following the service. Now mind you, many of our church members came from the South and by geography might have been presumed to have felt differently — but they did not. It was the "cultured," "educated," and "theologically liberal" who criticized us. While studying for a master's degree at Bradley University in the 1950s, I faced the unbelievable; our sociology class could only eat lunch at certain restaurants on a field trip because our black students were not allowed to eat in some restaurants! It was at that point that I decided to visit every black family in Peoria, Illinois, and write my master's thesis on the findings. A lady who was from the South, and who was my secretary for many years, still has a copy of that thesis, which she typed. She cherishes it not only because someone she cared for wrote it but also because as a Christian she could not ignore the truth of its findings. From time to time when I call her to see how she is doing, for we are both much older, she reminds me of how much work it was and how much we learned.

Poor communities that must rely on each other are different from those that do not have to rely on each other. Just as my railroad-track community was unique because everyone was equal by virtue of lack, other communities were different by virtue of possessions. The closer one gets to survival issues, the fewer social and political differences there are. The less one must be concerned for self-survival, the more time and resources are available for the "elective" issues. Each of our communities had possessions, some less measurable in dollars. There was an ethic to being without some material things, and in a strange way, this community took pride in "making do," in spite of it all. It built a strong, although sometimes strange, bond between the neighbors. I now understand why our struggling church shared a common bond with other struggling congregations, regardless of color. Those things in life that bind are always stronger than those things that separate. There are always more likenesses within us than differences between us.

We had all sorts of personality disorders in our community, as most do. It was not tolerance or kindness that permitted such; it simply was not noticed as being important. We certainly had our "crazies," but we didn't have the slightest idea about "personality disorders." I remember Joe. He was a grown man, at least as I recall him. Looking back from my current professional vantage point, I suspect that he would today be diagnosed as mentally retarded. He would certainly be diagnosed as abnormal. Joe would walk down the street with his overalls loosely hanging off his unshirted body, most often without shoes, singing "You Are My Sunshine" at the top of his lungs. He only knew the first few bars, and some of the words he sang were not correct, but he sang them over and over, followed by a mixture of nonsense words. The words he did not know were more than adequately compensated for by volume. He was always happy. People in the community never concerned themselves about him. It occurs to me that today surely some parent would fear for his or her child's safety and that every abuse or crime against a child in the city would be blamed on him. To my knowledge, he was peace loving and did no one harm.

There were other parts of my hometown. They varied from poverty far worse than ours to the very wealthy. The wealthy lived on the "West Side" of town. The middle class had secure jobs, usually with long-standing seniority, and were a bit better off. Their ethic allowed for a few more luxuries, but by and large they were frugal folk who maintained an honest work ethic and family value system. I didn't know the wealthy folks, but many of them were kind to me. I worked for them, and so did my father. There were several "culture ethic" communities in the one small city, as there are in all cities, towns, and villages.

We had one "Chinese" restaurant on the square downtown; I remember that it was oriental, but whether it was Chinese I do not know. We also had a Greek restaurant, on the square as well, on the ground floor right under the Lincoln Fiddle Shop, where I worked. I remember the Greek kids talking a strange language — one that I had no idea I would later in life learn in theological seminary.

Cultures that share sameness, and they all do, develop a common picture. It is not a photograph; that is too perfect. It is not a portrait; that is too individualistic. It is a caricature, a ludicrous and always exaggerated representation of the truth. However, that caricatured representation reveals the underlying message of truth about the intrinsic beliefs of that culture which are acted out in an extrinsic fashion.

Similarly, culture speaks to its intrinsic values in regard to food, water, housing, and the elements of physical survival. Food is not revered or, for that matter, in the United States often even appreciated. Buffets advertise "all you can eat," restaurants pile plates with more food than most are able to consume in one sitting, and more food is thrown away daily in many places than is eaten. We are grateful for those restaurants that donate fresh unsold food to the homeless rather than throwing it out, as many places do, to "avoid lawsuits." However, giving to the homeless what we would have thrown away does not expiate the sins of our culture ethic. The culture ethic is one of "we have worked for it, we pay the restaurant for it, and if we wish to buy it and throw it away, that's our business." This is true. And it is true because that is who we are. We firmly believe that we are not our brother's keeper. It is interesting that the "civilized" nations of the world are willing to spend unbelievable amounts of money to "protect" the less fortunate from tyranny, but we are unwilling to do more to feed them. Our priorities are indeed strange. The United States has been known to bomb countries, killing innocent people, in order to maintain our superpower status. It would be interesting to see what would happen if we undertook a war to build our superiority by kindness rather than killing.

Acting as we do is our cultural ethic, and we have every right to, and indeed cannot do other than, continue to display it. It is a sad but true observation that we cannot act otherwise no more than a zebra can change its stripes. The political, bureaucratic, economic, and personal empires are in motion, and just as the law of physics states, things in motion tend to continue in motion.

Several years ago while teaching for a West Coast university, I had the privilege of teaching a summer term in Hawaii, on the island of Maui. There were several students on that campus from Micronesia. These young folks revered their food, and it was truly awesome to observe them. They sat in silence as they ate with their bare hands. It was truly a religious experience. Each morsel was cherished; they did not take more than they could eat, and with each bite taken a prayer appeared to be spoken in silence. The direct physical contact with their food seemed to put them in touch with its source and the foundation of their existence. For these Micronesian students to eat with a metal knife, fork, and spoon would have been totally foreign to them and disgraced their culture ethic. Although they might have done so under force, their insides would have revolted.

This is what happens when we are forced to abandon our core — our ethic. We revolt. Our insides object in ways ranging from mental anguish to physical distress. Little do we know how much "mental illness," "cardiovascular disease," "family dysfunction," and numerous other twentieth-century ills are actually psycho-physiological revolts against being forced to live in opposition to a healthy ethic.

Our abuses of water, housing, and the other necessities of life are further revelations of our diseased core culture, our ethic. The fact that wonderful organizations such as Habitat for Humanity build houses for the homeless only indicts us that we should have to do so. A culture that cares for its own would not have degenerated to the point where such intervention is necessary. Polluting the streams, rivers, and oceans is not the disgrace — the disgrace is that we have a polluted culture, which extrinsically displays its intrinsic nature in this way. Herein lies the difference between ethic and ethics. True, our ethics stink in regard to the care of the earth. But if we stop our stinking, it will not change our culture; we must change our culture to stop our stinking. Only a radical change of our ethic can start to change the smell!

We know a great deal about intrinsic and extrinsic reward systems, as well as the power of the reward and punishment system. Behavioral modification is just that, a modification of behaviors. The substructure itself precipitates the behavior that needs changing. No amount of external change will restructure our culture. So long as we attempt to change "things," culture will remain unchanged. Minor adjustments to behavior will not affect the core and the seeds that dwell therein.

We must find a genuine understanding of and appreciation for life itself. Not the act of breathing, moving, or even thinking, but the essence of life and the power and importance of the soul. Without reverence for life, even our own existence is an egotistical sham that results from a delusional belief that there is something special about us that allows us to enjoy the creature comforts that others can only dream about.

Etiquette and manners are not culture. Some persons mistakenly think that a display of proper etiquette is a sign of "good culture." Not so. The reason we say "please" and "thank you" is not to show off what good parents we had or our social pedigree. It has to do with human dignity and the value of others and does not have to do with showing our level of education or sophistication. My father worked as a chauffeur, a hod carrier, a railroad worker, and a stable-man, (a friend of mine does that today and calls herself a "manure-meister!"). He had many jobs, but one couldn't really say he had an occupation. His lifelong "steady job" was working on the Wabash Railroad.

His work for the railroad was one of the best things of a material nature that he was able do for me. We got "passes" that allowed us to go to Chicago to see the museums and to St. Louis to enjoy the zoo, and we could visit our relatives in "St. Joe" during summer vacation. When it was time to head to New York State for college, I could have never afforded the train ride were it not for those passes.

In his jobs he often worked for bosses of a different color, and I remember that he always said "sir." Courtesy had to do with respect for them, not a display of his education. He probably did not learn that much etiquette with his fourth-grade education, but that's not what it was about. Courteous treatment of others has nothing to do with etiquette or "proper upbringing." It has to do with our respect of life. It has to do with our humility in the face of the value of others.

Culture as ethic is not adaptation. Adaptation is a manipulation, usually for the benefit of oneself. The ethic of culture is the *essence* of the group, society, or country that is displaying its ethics. Ethics are things that can more easily change. They are things we make up. We tend to have "ethics by intentionality." That is to say that we must have intention to effect the practice of ethic, which become ethics. For instance, fraud, in our culture, must have demonstrable intention to defraud to be indictable. Even if someone is hurt irreparably, if there was no intent to do it, our legal system can assign no guilt. This is why ethics are not core. It is why they are superficial and change with generations. Ethic is more permanent and has a basis that resides in the depths of soul, with or without intention of action. Ethics are not core, but only believed to represent the core — ethic. They are, therefore, in the true sense of the word, "artificial," meaning "reasonable facsimiles," but in truth they are "faux" representations. Like one's "faux mink" coat, everyone knows it is fake but treats it otherwise, lest we admit the truth. "Ethics" are not false because they are "man-made." They are false because they are incomplete, inaccurate, and biased representations of our true ethic.

Ethic as the soul of the society is much less malleable, but it can change. Sometimes it takes a war, an economic depression, a revolution, a reformation, or other cataclysmic event — but it can and does change. Culture as "ethic" is the nucleus of the societal cell, which has no choice but to express itself in both genetic and adaptive honesty. Human existence requires both adaptive and genetic honesty, that is, adaptive to live within others' rules and genetic in order to be authentic. Genetic honesty is easy — our DNA does that for us. Adaptive honesty is more difficult. When accomplished with everyone's good at heart, our adaptations do not transgress others. Fortunately, since so much is genetic, we do not often transgress ourselves.

2

Work and Vocation

Work is the purpose of the person,
not one's occupation or vocation.

This chapter is not about work ethics. Every profession has a code of ethics, that is, the expected behaviors of its members and the ramifications for ignoring them. Work is a four-letter word. In some minds, it is obscene, vulgar, and the result and expression of a curse, and therefore a curse word. True, the Old Testament history of work indicates that it was the result of disobedience in the Garden of Eden to God's commandment. However, was work not the "blessed curse" rather than the "cursed blessing"? Have you ever considered what life would be like, even in the Garden of Eden, with nothing to do but smell the roses? And although it might not have been called work, since there were only two persons on the earth, who would have picked the fruit, gathered daily food, or for that matter trimmed the rose bushes? Since work is the energy expended to accomplish something, are we to believe that had not "the curse" entered the picture, there would have been nothing to accomplish?

It is important that we understand the meaning of the word "work" within the context of the "curse." The condition of the human race is only slightly different from other creatures upon the earth. There is no indication that the other creatures did not have to toil constantly to find food and that they were immune to pain, in birthing or elsewhere. There is no indication that there was no pain in childbirth. The Bible states that the pain of childbirth would be "greatly multiplied." The announcement of God, in this case, is clearly one of putting the human race "in its place." And what is that place? If we are to believe the church fathers and the great creeds and confessions, the purpose of humans is to glorify God. How can that be done except by activity of some sort? And is that not work? Just as a child's work is play, all activity of the adult is purposeful and therefore work. Work must not be considered the curse. The curse is destructive activity, disrespect and blatant disregard for the total of creation, and our inability to recognize that much of what we do as "productive work" is actually existential annihilation. Life is full of the richness that has resulted from "work." The ethic of work allows us to find ourselves, relate to others, and participate in the culture of humanness, all of which is how humans glorify God.

Work is part of humanness. It is a necessity for being human, not the result of being human. There seems to be something just a little more human about those who must toil in the trenches than those who sit in ivory towers. There certainly is something more human about groveling for a day's wage than tapping into one's inheritance.

Work is creativity that results in duplication and proliferation of creation. The essential difference between human exertion of energy (work) and exertion of energy by a lower form of animal life is that animal work is primarily for survival of self and immediate offspring. Humans exert energy for a greater cause, a larger good. The human animal works not only to survive but with mission, purpose, and value. This cortical brain activity is physiologically and culturally different from lower species that do not possess frontal lobes.

These brain parts give us "executive" function — the ability to make judgment calls, organize, plan, and behave in a socially acceptable fashion.

Work is one of the values that are learned early in life. Children learn work as they play. They do not understand that their work is joy and that their joy is work. Adults speak of the drudgery of work and for the most part fail to find joy in it. Work as a human endeavor has many phases, each with its own value and enjoyment. It is important to recognize and appreciate the importance of each step for its own unique importance and not to wait until the end to experience the joy.

The first phase is the vision, that is, the idea and image of what is to be done. The creative mind finds excitement in the contemplation, the planning, the constructive argumentation of directions of action, and the anticipation of dream fulfillment. The second phase is assembling the parts, the pieces, the people, the team, the finances, the organization, and all the material aspects necessary. The fulfillment of this phase brings heightened excitement, and the sense of accomplishment swells as we move from dream to reality. The third phase is the construction. Whether the construction is physical, mental, or otherwise, the externalization of the internal image brings tangible proof of accomplishment. The fourth phase is completion of the task. This phase is rewarding and fulfilling, but to the creative and productive mind it is always a mixture of joy and anticipation of the next project. Work fulfilled must always result in more work to be done or the basic reason for the work is lost. In that loss are to be seen some of the world's worst tragedies. Parents who have successfully reared children regularly divorce because they have fulfilled and are no longer fulfilling. Churches that have sacrificed to build beautiful sanctuaries lose the bond of struggle and begin haggling and often splinter. Sometimes the joy is in the pursuit, not the capture.

Work is procreativity that results in the reproduction of life. The simple physiological reproduction of living cells is not unique to the human. This work goes on in every form of life from the one-celled amoeba to humans. The essential element to understand is that each species can only reproduce itself and the life that is germane to it. The amoeba cannot reproduce a multiple-celled offspring, and the human cannot produce an amoeba. As simple and mundane as it may sound, the issue is important: that is, life produces like life. The work of the human is part and parcel of this process, and just as the amoeba's work is to produce more amoebae with the task of continuing to reproduce amoebae, the human does likewise. Work therefore has a core in the genetic substrate of the species, and in the case of the human, the real work is producing humans with all the capacity of the human and the work that comes from that entity. Although the expression of that core may differ from bricklayer to lawyer, the real work of the human race does not change because of job or profession.

Work is the foundation for thought and thinking. Many persons believe that ***you are what you do,*** including Hillman in his book ***The Soul's Guide*** (p. 252). I would assert that this is the opposite of true. Instead, ***we do what we are.*** It is true that we make changes as a result of our work, but these tend to be single actions rather than core changes in the person. There may be exceptions; however, there are no exceptions to the fact that as our person changes so does our work. Work is the expression of our thinking and gives rise to further thinking that in turn changes who we really are. This reciprocal mental process allows for growth and productivity simultaneously.

In my own experience, it was the men in my life who taught me the value and the joy of work. I am certain that, like all of us, they must have griped and complained from time to time about their work; however, it is interesting that

I do not remember that part. My grandfather, who was at various times a carpenter, cabinetmaker, bricklayer, steeplejack, and at times practiced a variety of other trades, always seemed to enjoy his work and made it enough fun that I wanted to help him. I remember my father working more than any man should have to, but I never remember him complaining about it. He was always grateful to have the work and somehow found the energy to go to an evening job when the day job was done. Work had meaning: life and the ability to give to his children opportunities he never had, like graduating from high school. My father had a fourth-grade education and my mother a sixth. Since education is now taken for granted, today's generation is given money and material possessions, gifts of far lesser value than was the gift of education. No doubt work had a very different meaning to them than it did to the generations that would come after them.

Persons who get caught in the rut of becoming what they do stagnate and eventually find themselves at the end of a dead-end street. These persons mistake vocation for work. They do not realize that vocation is simply the method they have chosen to "make a living," that is, earn money. As a result, their "work" is not productive. It only makes money and possibly pleases a boss. Its deepest purpose is never realized. They no longer grow. They no longer think creatively. They no longer have a vision. They are deadlocked into believing that their job is their person. They have become their work rather than their work becoming them. They are the most wonderful employees that an employer can have. They never have ideas, so they never cause trouble. They no longer yearn for a better life, so they do nothing to "get ahead." They are grateful for whatever is handed to them, because they know that is their worth, so they never seek a raise in pay. The problem is theirs and theirs alone. They live the life of mediocrity at best, are hardly distinguishable from the machines in the shop, do what they are told without question, and retire to "enjoy" the rest of their life. However, they are unable to do so. They have never thought, been creative, asserted themselves, or led even their own emotions, and now, behold, in their retirement they need someone to tell them what to do on a daily basis. They have lived a life of drudgery for the majority of their years and now believe they have paid their dues in order to enjoy the few retirement days that are left in their life. Unless we have been productive, we can no more enjoy retirement than a machine can enjoy its non-motion after it has been turned off.

Of course, the major reason is that productive persons never really retire; they simply trade in one kind of productivity for another. We speak today of the "work ethic" as if it is some kind of a strange mutation of living persons. The reason we have a "work ethic" is because the ethic of work is the basis of life. The core of our existence is how and where we spend our energy.

Work cannot be drudgery and also be nutritive to the soul. The spending of our energy is the expression of our being. It cannot at one and the same time be drudgery and also be nutritive to ourselves and to other souls. I have had the incredibly good fortune to have had to work my entire life and pay my way since long before high school, and I have had few jobs that I did not enjoy, and even some I have come to appreciate for what I learned from them. I have never had an occupation that I did not enjoy. There have been aspects of and times in some jobs, that is, individual parts of occupations, that were not enjoyable, but I could return today to any occupation that I have ever had and thoroughly enjoy doing it again.

Too many people confuse the lack of pain with enjoyment. True enjoyment frequently has a price to pay, and sometimes that is pain, either physical or mental or both.

Smashing my finger in the three-point hookup on my tractor is hardly enjoyable. However, if I am on my way outside to grade the driveway and know that I may potentially smash my finger, I can still look forward to the greater part of this task — the fresh air, hearing the wildlife, and driving the tractor. If I smash my finger, that comes with the territory.

Work is the promise of life and living. Being entrusted with valuable things gives one purpose. To be trusted with money, machines, management of workers, people's lives, people's food, and fellow humans' welfare is truly the promise of life and living. Without this work, we would have no one responsible for our living and we would be responsible for no one else's. Such isolation and total independence would be destructive to the mind, body, and relationships that are essential for our survival.

Work is the stage upon which the human drama is played. As we fulfill our roles in life, each of us has a stage. We are the principal actor, the prima donna, the agonist and antagonist, the victor and the victim. We cannot separate ourselves from the process, and we cannot separate the process from ourselves.

There are two or more sides to every person. In persons suffering from schizophrenia, the sides are pronounced, and often both sides deviate from reality. In persons not so mentally afflicted, there are also at least two sides, which we call roles; however, each side portrays a part of the person, and both or all sides are in touch with reality, just different aspects of reality. The book *Mother Teresa,* by Anne Sebba (Doubleday, New York, 1997), reveals both the popular and the not so complimentary side of this 1979 Nobel Peace Prize recipient.

It could be argued that her rigid and less charitable side was inconsistent with what she was doing as a person of mercy. However, I would argue that such is not the case. In fact, I would argue that both were necessary for her to accomplish the expression of her inner person, since she was her work and her work was not her. For instance, the story is told of her stopping the feeding of an infant in mid-meal if the prayer bell tolled. She would immediately attend to the prayer bell rather than continue with her act of mercy. She had no choice. Her person was based upon a philosophical base that was psychologically and spiritually genetic. To not pay attention to the prime source of her strength, or to ignore the food for her soul, would have been to transgress her own person and as a result change the direction of her work. It is also recounted that she was intolerant when luxury ways of life were introduced and literally threw them out the window. It could be argued that at least she could have given those items (washing machines, etc.) to needy persons. Again, I would argue that she could not do otherwise and be true to her "person as the work." If she wanted to address her life as the result of her work, she could have acted differently. This is not to support antisocial behavior. It is to note that we are our work — it is *the* expression of who we are, not *an* expression of who we are. To argue further, Hitler could have changed elements of his dictatorship and perhaps a few persons may have been helped or at least saved from his hellish regime. But that would not have changed who he was — he was his work. Changing a few or even many acts within his lifetime would not have changed who he was.

In most persons, there are distinctly different behaviors present in their "work" and in their home environments. However, when studied in depth psychologically or spiritually, these apparent differences are minute and superficial. One's manner of handling conflict, ability to deal with stress, utilization of inner resources, and other aspects of human living which are deep within the soul are not very different from one location to the other. There may be a bit more freedom to "act out" in one setting over the other, but the physiological management of external pressure is handled internally very much the same. Further, I would assert that the "acting out" differs only in its method, not in its purpose.

Our actions are the results, and the results are our actions. The stage is us, and we are the stage. Everyone is watching, and we are watching everyone. We are the audience, and the audience is us. Just as when we look into a mirror it reflects a smaller image than is actually present, when we look into the mirror of life, the reflection is smaller than life.

Work is the basis for dealing with both life and death. The beginning of life and the ending of life are still the greatest mysteries to the human race. We cannot account for the miracle of cell mitosis that develops the genetic code into a viable breathing, moving, thinking organism. Neither can we understand that final stage in this earthly pilgrimage which we call death. The work that we have done is nonetheless important at both ends. The work we have exerted to become the person we are doubtless offers a basis for our offspring, and the work of who we become is that which follows us long after we take our last breath. Shakespeare was poetic but only half correct when he stated: "The evil that men do lives after them; the good is oft interred with their bones" (*Julius Caesar,* Scene II, in *The Complete Works of William Shakespeare,* Crown Publishers, 1955). The truth is that both the good and the evil live after us, and both play a part in that which we produce and in the offspring whom we reproduce.

Work is that which ties the past to the present and things past and present to the future. The continuum of life is possible through the medium of work. It is a bridge from idea to action, from action to completion, from conceptualization to realization, and from primordial beginnings to sophisticated endings. We build upon that which the work of others has left us, and we leave work products for those who come after us to build upon.

Work is the purpose of the person, not the vocation or occupation. Many persons choose a given "profession" in the belief that the functions of vocational choice will provide purpose and meaning. Rarely is this the case. Instead, if the person does not find the "work" ego-syntonic (as psychologists would call it), that is, internally compatible with one's self, the profession becomes only a job and becomes drudgery rather than fulfillment. Sometimes the words vocation, occupation, profession, and job are used interchangeably. They are not the same. While vocation and profession may have similarities, and vocation and occupation have likenesses, the psychological differences are huge. Persons who see themselves as having purpose rarely have a "job." They project themselves into a purpose for their exertion of energy. The bricklayer who perceives the laying of bricks as a "job" is not nearly as likely to build a beautiful fireplace as the one who sees laying bricks as a profession. Pride, a sense of purpose, and a resulting interest in the results rather than just seeing that the "job" is done make for work that is the essence of the person, rather than a task performed by a person.

Work is the completed task of human existence — the ultimate earthly way to love God and others as oneself. When all is said and done, how would we measure, perceive, or relate to anyone except as we experience, observe, and participate in the exertion of energy, i.e., work, by others? It is the flag we fly, the bumper sticker we wear, the *imago viva* of every aspect of who we are.

Work became the opportunity for most of us to find our way in life. At age ten, I was privileged to apprentice with a fine human being whom I shall never forget, a German fiddle maker. Raleigh Garrett was unusual in many ways. He was very charitable, fixed folks' musical instruments for their children when they did not have money, and was always cheerful. I remember that he had two thumbs on his right hand and used both of them! Years later, a fire in the Greek restaurant below his shop, as I recall it being reported, destroyed several stores as well as the Lincoln Fiddle Shop. Even as a grown man, I cried when I heard that terrible news. Later, when I visited Raleigh, I learned that he had cried too; the shop had been his life, and those fiddles were part of his family. He was a rare individual who saw something in me that I did not see in myself. He paid me $2.00 a week and a music lesson (which was very good pay in 1938) to learn to make violins, repair instruments, and sweep the floor. I remember my father going with me to ask for that job. Mr. Garrett looked me over and asked me some questions, most of which I do not remember. He told my father that I was "awfully young" and that I'd have to work hard. Both were true. I do remember that I told him that I did not like school (and that was the truth!) and that I wanted to learn to play the trumpet. He gave me a gray denim apron and taught me the rudiments of violin making, repairing brass instruments, trumpet playing, and sweeping floors! That kind of work can hardly be considered a curse.

Work for most of us provided the first rung on the ladder to a better life. For many of my childhood years, we did not have an indoor toilet. My parents did not have a bathtub until my first summer home from college, at which time I helped to install it. We appreciated the iron-rich well water that tasted cool and fresh as we drank out of the common tin cup that hung on the pump. The pump was at the end of a long lot, and I am told that as a small child I went there to "pout"!

It was work that provided the wherewithal to climb beyond the ignorance that such a life would have inflicted. Work was seen as a blessing and the only way to "get ahead." Although I was not personally encouraged to continue in school beyond about the eighth grade, it was clear to me that education and work were twins, and that without education, I would end up doing a very different kind of work. Even at that, staying in school was hit or miss. To me, work was seen as so valuable that it seemed far more important most of the time than going to school. Work produced immediate results. You could see the results and count the money. School was something that was called "an education," and if you were lucky when you got done, you might get a job.

However, the purpose of work is not primarily intended to better us economically or even intellectually. Its purpose is to better us spiritually. It provides for the development of soul, the expression of love, and the hope that undergirds self-actualization and transcendence. Most persons view "work" as drudgery, negative, something one "must" do, and something that everyone looks forward to "retiring" from. Why do we look forward to discontinuing that which is the essence of who we are?

Work allows us to leave something behind that proves we were here. We all struggle to leave something that others will recognize as "us." To lose forever one's identity is threatening to most humans. To find something with someone's name on it establishes connections and continuity of life. I recall lifting the lid of a large wooden toolbox long after my grandfather had died and seeing "John B. Johnson" scrawled with a broad-point carpenter's pencil on the inside of the lid. All of a sudden, that grandfather who taught me how to cut angles, help build staircases, and saw on a straight line with a handsaw was alive again. Identity with one's work is so primary that artists sign their work and clothing designers proudly ask us to pay to wear their signatures!

The excitement among archeologists and anthropologists when they can identify remains, ruins, and antiquities is not hard to understand. They are projecting the recognition they hope their own legacies will find and can be sure that those who left the artifacts hoped so as well, since markings were left for identification.

Surroundings become the frame for the picture of work. I have a friend who lives in a geodesic dome. For many years, there was no running water, no electricity, and a Spartan almost hermit sense to his life-style. He is an artist, and a very fine one. His work spoke of his atmosphere and had a distinct signature to it. His work is still beautiful but has a different signature due to the changed surroundings for his artistic soul. The artwork of the master painters, the music of the masters, and the sculpture of the stone masters changed over their lifetimes. Often it is thought of as the development of the artist. And, to be sure, it is that, but that development cannot be separated from the surroundings, the frame in which that work is created. I have no doubt that the addition of creature comforts, although he should not be deprived of them, has changed my friend's artistic expressions forever, not for the worse, not for the better, only changed.

Existence is work. It doesn't matter where that existence occurs. While attending a professional convention in New York City, I ate at the famous Stage Door Café, where sandwiches are obscene in their generosity. Since all I could eat was half a sandwich, it seemed utterly sinful to send the other delicious half back to the kitchen to be thrown away, I wrapped it neatly, and as I walked down the street among homeless persons begging for money and rummaging through garbage cans, I offered the sandwich to several beggars. One after another refused the sandwich, even when I explained where I had gotten it. One man said to me, "What do you think I am, a beggar?" He refused the sandwich and returned to digging through the garbage!

Homelessness itself can become work. It is the work of the homeless. Sometimes their work is to refuse food, shelter, and health care. To accept these comforts, even necessities of life, would destroy their way of life. As hard as this is to understand, it is understandable. To accept my sandwich did not offer the promise of hope of anything more. It did not offer a way to change the next meal or the next day. To continue to dig in the garbage gave continuity of work and the promise of the ability to continue that way of life tomorrow.

Homelessness is not only a condition of living, it is a phenomenon. It has always been with us and surely always will be. It has become particularly apparent in the United States in recent years because it seems so alien to our obvious affluence.

3

Play and Recreation

Play is the sunshine of the soul
shining upon the stage of life.

Play is genderless. Play is ageless. Play is work. Work is play. Play is life. Life is play. The human race began, as it is recorded in the Christian Bible, in a garden where play was the order of the day. We speak of dying and going to a dreamland where all is joy and light and where there are no tears, no pain, and no work — a place of play. Play is the sunshine of the soul shining upon the stage of life.

We think of play as including laughter, giggles, joy, friendship, teamwork, games, winning, losing, and learning the lessons of life all within the context of fun. And that is all true, and much more. Play is the way a child puts life to its test. It is the way the child learns rules, the consequences of breaking rules, the limits of selfishness, and the values of sharing. Play has no limit to the number of simultaneous players — from one to infinity.

As adults, we refer to play as recreation. We literally search for ways to return to the innocence of the world of play. We speak of vacation as time for play and rejuvenation. Just as "juvenile" speaks of youth, so does "rejuvenate." We are constantly seeking ways to return to a time in life when we can learn in innocence. Play has automatic forgiveness for every "mistake." Play keeps no score. It is only when the seriousness of industry and business takes over play, as in professional sports, that play ceases to be play and becomes a vocation used for making money, not learning life.

Play is the child's work because it is the medium through which a child can utilize progressive development to learn how to get to the next stage. This process does not change throughout our lifetimes. Our play is our work, and our work is our play — both for the sole purpose of moving us on to the next stage of our existence. Play is seen as imaginative, fantasy, mythical, and mystical, and yet we are reminded of Freud's *Beyond the Pleasure Principle,* which clearly shows the purpose of pleasure and that its purpose is far more than play.

Play is always a process of learning. Putting toys together, watching how things move, observing toys functioning properly, and seeing toys break are all part of learning how play will work out and how work will play out.

Long before we learn that there is an academic subject called physics, we have learned the basics of leverage, the inclined plane, the force of gravity, and much more. Long before we can count or know the meaning of numbers, we know if we are missing one of our jacks or toy soldiers. Long before we can spell, we know that "b-l-o-c-k" is different from "d-o-l-l."

My childhood, like that of most kids of my day, was filled with the "University of Play as Work." Although I did very poorly in school, I have no doubt that the education received on my neighborhood street has stood me in good stead. During a visit to my childhood hometown after becoming an adult, I drove under a huge railroad trestle, many feet above the road, that spanned a river. As I drove under it, I recalled that I had often walked that trestle with other kids. Although it pains me to admit my childhood stupidity, more than once we had to climb over the side and cling to the metal ladders on the side in order to avoid oncoming trains. They were Wabash trains (the "Banner Blue" and the "Blue Bird"), the same railroad my father worked for. Sometimes a child's play is dangerous, yet the play aspect of the activity obliterates common sense.

The Herkermer Street Circus was always a great event when I was a kid. The street we lived on, Grand Avenue, was formerly known as Herkermer Street, as I was told by the older kids, and surely they knew the truth! Every summer, we kids worked like beavers to put together the circus named after that street. There were several sources of raw materials for this circus. My grandfather brought home the old electrical wiring from buildings torn down, and the Disney kids' dad had an auto mechanic garage across the alley from us where we got old tires, batteries, and all sorts of good junk for a circus. Then, of course, there were our pets. The dogs and cats were great! There was also Mrs. Mammen, who lived on the corner and owned a really beautiful parrot that she kept in a great big handsome cage for everybody to see. One summer that beautiful bird got out of the cage, and I remember that it flew up into the huge tree in our front yard. I don't think I ever knew whether or not she got it back. Then there were the Schweinboldts, who had a rock and flower garden that was the envy of everyone on the street. They had a car and traveled across United States and brought back beautiful rocks from everywhere. On circus day (and at other times), folks would walk through their yard and "ooh and aah" with plenty of good reason. Mr. Grundyke always had literally dozens of beautifully painted whirligig ornaments in his yard that he had made out of wood. They were painted red, white, green, and all sorts of colors, and many of them moved in all kinds of ways in the wind. People took pride in their yards and their gardens. On circus day, they all showed them off.

The dogs were taught to jump through tires that hung from tree limbs. We guys learned to jump through them too, and we could clear more tires than the best dog! There was a distinct gender-based code of behavior. Girls did not jump through tires and boys did not try to dance on their tippy-toes and act like ballet dancers. I am not aware that we thought that boys were better or worse than girls, but we had no doubt that we were different, and there were some things that boys just didn't do and some things that girls just didn't do. The boys bowed when applauded and the girls curtsied. Wasn't that what was supposed to happen?

I remember winning the prize for being able to go headfirst through the most hanging tires. There was also a high wire made of braided old electric wire, thanks to my grandfather. I don't remember how high it was because that was one act that I did not do. We sold apples, lemonade, and shiny "good-luck buckeyes." The McElvoys, a Catholic family with eight kids that lived next door, made homemade root beer every year and always broke out a few gallons for the occasion. I don't remember making any money or what happened to it if we did. I suspect now in retrospect, however, that the older kids got their fare share. By the time I was one of the "older kids," I was fully employed at real work.

Such ingenuity! I suspect that many of our ideas were borrowed from the "Jitney Suppers" that our grade schools held each year to raise money. They would have cake walks, coin tosses, and all sorts of innocuous gaming, with the full intent of losing so the school could win. I suspect that the families on our street saw our circus in much the same light.

It is difficult to think of children who somehow today cannot find "fun" in the simple things of life. Grandpa's old electric wiring, hooked up to one of the Disney kids' dad's old batteries, boosted by an old magneto from a Model T Ford, plus a couple of tin cans, made a great telephone. We buried the wire from one yard to the next. There were only two really serious problems that we never overcame. We couldn't figure out a way to make a bell ring next door and we couldn't invent a way to "dial someone up." But such problems were not insurmountable — we just yelled down the street and told them to pick up their "phone"! I learned a lot from that experience, especially from the first shock I got from that magneto!

When one views today's supermarkets of toys, it is both enviable and pitiable. The technology and the inventiveness in children's toys are truly incredible. For that, children should be grateful. They can learn so much from "educational" toys. However, by the same token, many of these children will never learn the value of their own inventiveness and reap the rewards of success. Making a "rubber gun" out of a broomstick and slices of an old inner tube and creating a doll out of household items brought a joy of learning to the child that cannot be provided by a purchased toy.

In order for our circus and our telephone company to work, we had to figure out how to advertise them, so we decided to publish a neighborhood paper. There was a lady who collected all sorts of botanical things, and although I can't remember her name, I'm sure she was richly rewarded. She had whole rooms full of leaves and things she had collected and pressed between newspapers. She took a special interest in us; I think she was a schoolteacher, although if she was, I was never in her class. She encouraged us kids to do all kinds of creative and educational things, including develop the newspaper. This was quite a difficult task. We had to have moveable type, some kind of a press, ink, and paper. I do not remember where we got the ink or the paper. I do remember that we found a one-gallon coffee can in which we carefully centered a piece of pipe through each end and then filled with concrete. The Disney kids' dad soldered tin "type holders" into which we could insert our rubber letters. We had to have something that would roll so we could print one line at a time because we didn't have enough rubber letters for two lines at a time. Then we would ink it up, roll it onto a piece of paper, and *voilà* — we produced the first line, the title of our great neighborhood *Herkermer Street News*! I don't remember just how many issues we printed, although I suspect it was precious few and maybe only one, but I learned a tremendous amount about both work and play, to say nothing about time, money, people, and life in general. The thing I remember most was the encouragement we received from our elders. They surely doubted that we could pull it off, but they certainly never told us so and even helped find the "tools" for us to try to do it.

The support of the community was unreal. People took pride in the kids, and when we got into trouble, a price was extracted by more than just our parents. There was no hesitancy in those days to help "straighten out" someone else's child. It was expected. Play was a part of life, and we took it seriously.

Play always has meaning. Pleasure is the "milk and honey" of life; however, the thin line between pain and pleasure tells us that there is no specific point at which work becomes play or play becomes work or at which we can tell exactly when the pleasure stops and the pain begins. I have always been interested in observing someone with a hangnail or skin lesion. The person will invariably pick at it, even though it hurts, because somewhere in there is pleasure.

Play is lighthearted, laughter filled, and is characterized by the jester, the clown, or the dunce. Deep within each of these there is anything but fun. The lightheartedness is to disguise the depression, the jest is but a covering for hostility, the clown is a caricature of sorrow, and the dunce is pitied stupidity.

One of my favorite pastimes has been to watch the Three Stooges. Their idiocy and stupidity are rivaled only by their portrayal of the clumsy, maladroit oaf in all of us. Their "comic relief" is exactly that — a relief for us from our own not-so-comical human foibles. Slapstick comedy and the sophisticated embarrassment of Charlie Chaplin and other silent movie stars are simply our lives projected in real time. Play was living — and living was play — all simply portrayed by someone else so that we could laugh at them without crying inside about ourselves.

William Shakespeare said that all humor is tragic. That is doubtless true. Our jokes are at someone else's expense, our humor rarely is about ourselves, and our solace is in somebody else's suffering. The "play" is the embodiment of truths that cannot be said elsewhere. The stage is a real way to artificially project our lives into real time in an unreal fashion. The actors are sufficiently like us, yet by virtue of makeup and acting skill distanced from us, so that we can see ourselves at play-work without knowing it is us!

Masks, costumes, accents, music, makeup, props, choreography, and much more allow us to truly project ourselves into another sphere, called theater — play/work — without admission of guilt or ownership of the outcome. There is absolutely no difference between this and the child's world of play/work. The child is allowed to fantasize and live in an unreal world. Adults are not supposed to do so (but we do so anyway!).

I vividly remember our eldest daughter living in such a world as a small child. We lived in an older home with a huge attic. She would go to the attic and wrap herself in a curtain as if dressing as a bride and come bouncing down the stairs singing her child's version of "Here Comes the Bride." At other times, she would line up her dolls on the stairs and lecture them, and they would talk back. What a life! The greater question is why did we give it up when we grew up, or did we? And if we did, why did we? Or to reckon with the truth — we did not give it up, cannot give it up, and shall never give it up.

We are intrigued with the magical quality of much music. Wonderful pieces such as "Peter and the Wolf" pique the child within us, yet we are able to express it with the skills learned from childhood to maturity. Poetry and prose do likewise. Poems like "The Night Before Christmas" are quoted and thoroughly enjoyed by children and adults alike. The multi-billion-dollar novel industry, harlequin or otherwise, is built upon the fact that our play is our work and our work is our play. Fantasy, imagination, the mystical, and the mythical cannot be separated from any aspect of our life. That's why all of life is play, and play is all of life.

4

Homes and Houses

*Home is a place in the heart —
and the heart in a place.*

Home is not a place. It is not a house. It is not a room. It is not a town, city, or village. It is not a mansion or even the most humble abode. Home is an emotional state. The perception of "home" is unique and highly individualistic. I have been a guest in the homes of the rich and the poor, in the United States and many countries of the world, including Third World countries. Sometimes a palatial house is not a home. Sometimes (most always) a run-down shack is a home. I have been the guest of "primitive" people in Third World countries, where the fire burned in the doorway of the hut at night to keep the animals out, and I have never been in one that was not a home.

It always interests me to see pictures and read stories of tours through people's fancy homes to raise money for various projects. Most often these are tours thorough *houses* to raise money for people who already have *homes.* The people who tour these houses also have their own *houses,* but may not have *homes.* The money raised is often used to help the "needy," who have *homes* but not *houses.* The people who have homes but not houses need to be thankful. The people who have houses but not homes need to be pitied — for most of them do not know it. There are, of course, many people who have both houses and homes. They need to be especially thankful.

There are so many different kinds of "homes." Watching the "homeless" in any large city gives one a new perspective on what makes a home or, for that matter, even a house.

I was sitting in Union Station in our nation's capital early one Saturday morning, the day before Mother's Day, slowing savoring an Au Bon Pan® coffee on my way to a meeting paid for by an organization with a lot of money. I noticed an elderly woman enter pushing an ingeniously concocted grocery cart. To make it easier to push the cart over curbs, she had two bicycle wheels attached to the sides with wire. The cart held two umbrellas, many plastic bags, and heaven only knows what else. I was reminded that there are many kinds of homeless people. I wondered just why she was homeless. Some of the homeless look like they just "fell over the edge." So many people in our country live "right on the edge," and it takes only something small to push them over. By the looks of her well-organized cart, this elderly woman had fallen over the edge some time ago.

Nonetheless, she looked like somebody's mother. A wedding band made me wonder if she was somebody's widow. She dug for nickels, dimes, and pennies to buy a bagel and looked for cups of coffee or sodas that people did not completely drink. I wondered where and how she had even gotten the loose change. She could fill the cup with a small bit of coffee left in it with lots of cream and sugar from the condiment cart.

I could not help but think of my early days in college when more than once I counted out pennies — fifty-four of them to be exact — for spaghetti and meat sauce at a tiny, old-fashioned Italian diner in downstate New York.

I watched this woman, as did everyone else — something was different about her. She read a *Washington Post* that someone had left behind, and she softly spoke to a custodial worker in Spanish and to another in English. While many of the homeless are mentally ill, on drugs, or alcoholics, she displayed no obvious clinical signs of any of these things. She was a montage of manners, demeanor, and an obvious cultural and even educational background, covered with a well-worn, wrinkled, and dirty plastic raincoat.

After finding a nearly full cup of coffee a hurried commuter had left behind, she went back for a second bagel. She counted her pennies several times but couldn't come up with enough. As the cashier — and everyone else in line — became more and more impatient, I could not help but pay for her bagel. I left not knowing who she was — nor did she know who I was, but at some level we both learned something more about those who have and those who have not.

Thomas Moore, in his book *The Re-Enchantment of Daily Life* (Harper Collins, New York, 1940, p. 77), states that "Home is an emotional state, a place in the imagination where feelings of security, belonging, placement, family, protection, memory, and personal history abide." He is right. It is the work of the person, not the person's work, that makes a house a home.

Most parents want their house to be a home. We put pictures on the walls, hang family photos all over the place, and keep worn-out pieces of furniture, because it makes us feel "at home." I can remember with considerable pain that day when I came home from school and found my mother sitting on a straight wooden chair crying. I knew why before I entered the house, because I saw the coals from our stove on the snow in the front yard. The furniture store had repossessed our furniture, including the pot-bellied stove that we relied on for heat. There remains to this day the one surviving piece of furniture from that unfortunate purchase. In front of a couch in our library sits that coffee table with a glass top and an engraved lion on the wood under the glass. I was told, and I recall, since I was about eight years old when my folks bought the furniture "on time," that I fell in love with the carving on the coffee table and the salesman "gave" it to us. I suspect my parents paid for it many times over, but nonetheless, it could not be repossessed since they owed nothing on it. I was told that I had to understand, because there was no money to make the monthly payment. Everything in our community in those days was bought "on time." It was a sure way for poverty to beget greater poverty, but it is all people seemed to know how to do. I guess in truth that this method doesn't differ that much from a whole generation of Americans who misuse credit cards. Even groceries were often bought that way from a local store that I'm sure charged the proverbial arm and leg. However, the store was also known to forgive debts from time to time. Dombrowski's grocery store, which allowed credit, was our only hedge against hunger more than once. I also remember that at year's end they gave away those garish calendars covered all over with silver and gold flecks. I'm not sure whether those expensive-looking gifts were meant to make up for something.

Moving is so common in our society that is has become the norm. However, picking up one's things and moving is no less traumatic today than it ever was. My wife lived in one home from birth to college. I was not as fortunate; however, by today's standards, my life was really very stable. I only lived in four houses from birth to college. That's fewer moves than my own children have had to make! Relocating offers advantages in some respects because our children must learn the *modus operandi* of today's society; however, this rationalization sounds like another cop-out. Stability still offers greater opportunity for the inner spirit to grow than does constantly having to put internal growth on "hold" while so many externals are in flux.

Home is very difficult to build, but even more difficult to dismantle. I have been part of more than one situation where an elderly person has had to decide what to sell, what to give away, what to throw away, and what to keep when moving into a nursing home or retirement setting. "Things" are important not only because they have beauty or are functional. They are important because they are extensions of "home." The chair with the broken-down seat may look useless, but it fits our broken-down body that molded it as our body broke over many years. It is not a "chair." It is "the place where I sit when I am home."

I have been observer to more than one unfortunate marital dissolution. Breaking up housekeeping is far more difficult than setting up housekeeping. It is always interesting and amazing what material things have become of value to the partners who are splitting up. All of the sudden their "home" becomes a collection of "things" that belong to "you" or to "me." Things accumulated together must belong to some "one." This is only one reason why it is possible to get a divorce but impossible to get unmarried. Parts of every relationship we have ever had remain with us forever. The marital pair can frame their divorce decree just as they probably did not frame their wedding license, but what do they do with the children, the relatives, the "things," the common friends, the memories, and so many other "non-disposables"?

I guess the integration of life and the accumulation of things is what makes for "homemaking" as opposed to "housekeeping." Housekeeping is the keeping of things, whereas homemaking is exactly that, making a home.

Most of us accumulate far more than we need over a lifetime. However, if you want a tough job, go through your house and ask yourself what is part of your "home" and what is not. Some things we don't need — it would seem. However, that otherwise useless item given to us by a dear friend is part of our "home," and the house would be less a home without it. To make our house a "home" requires that more than we alone live there. Our relatives, our friends, and yes, sometimes even our enemies also live in our home in things they have given to us. Memories are connected to people, places, and things. Memories are the links that allow our chains of life to have continuity, congruity, and meaning.

It is often sad to see older folks who move to what they consider will be their "last home." They give away, sell, and throw away everything they can. They never expect to move again. They keep the bare necessities — only the things to help them die. At that point, they must, and they do, transfer their feelings of "home" into memories of the past and beliefs about the afterlife. It is no surprise that when Jesus was teaching about such things, he told his followers, "In my father's house there are many mansions." He did not speak of possessions, activity, or anything else. He promised a "home" — the anchor spot in everyone's life where one looks for nurturing, shelter, food, and rest.

Home is a place in the heart — and the heart in a place.

5

Learning and Education

Learning is a life-long process –
the question is not whether we will learn,
but what we will learn.

The ethic of learning is not for what we can know but for what we can learn. Knowledge is never complete — we are all lifetime learners. We are never in a state of "know" but always in a state of "knowing." Life is always in the gerund form, a verb form functioning as a noun. Knowing is the gerund form of life. The brain is a repository of knowledge rather than the soul of intelligent living. The brain is our computer, but with infinitely more memory. The brain, like the computer, is incapable of utilizing knowledge except by human direction.

There is a model of education that assumes the brain to be an empty cranium, and the job of educators is to fill it. I remember a poem, but haven't the foggiest idea what it is called, that went something like this: "Ram it in, cram it in, little heads are hollow; slam it in, cram it in, there is still more to follow."

The great philosophers from time immemorial have debated the relationship of nature and nurture. The brain has been seen as everything from a blank slate (*tabla rasa*) to another muscle in the body that grows with exercise. Although there is no doubt truth in most of these approaches, they mostly avoid discussing the real value of the brain — and that is in its capacity for learning. The "theories" address the results of learning as methods for promoting various educational approaches. We now know that there is no one correct method of education and that everyone learns in a unique fashion. Although these were called methods of learning, they were not. They were methods for training and assumed the human to be another kind of animal that could be sent to "training school" and come out with the desired behavior and knowledge.

The ethic of learning is the ethic of being teachable. There is no teacher, and there is no learner. There are only learners who are simultaneously teachers and teachers who are simultaneously learners. As one who taught the trumpet for many years, I can attest that no one can be *taught* to play a trumpet (or any other instrument). One can, however, be taught to teach oneself. There is a critical and important difference between these two seemingly similar statements. As a teacher, it is assumed that one is dishing out the information and the other is consuming it. All teachers know that is not so. Instead, as we teach we learn about the learner, about ourselves, and about the material being taught. The learner also learns about himself or herself, about the teacher, and about the material. Then, in the imitation of all that, the learner teaches himself or herself that body of knowledge. The skills to carry out that body of knowledge, as in the case of playing the trumpet, are the external manifestations of the internalized knowledge that has been self-taught.

All good teachers will tell you that they learned far more from their teaching than any of their students did. The highway of learning across a teacher's desk is in both directions. Teachers who assume they have unlearned pupils sitting in front of them soon learn that the pupils know a great deal about many things that they as teachers do not know. The students, hopefully, come to recognize the same thing about their teacher.

We must keep in mind the difference between a leader and a teacher. All great teachers have basically been leaders. A teacher assumes correctness of the information offered and believes that he or she can "teach it" to those who do not know it. The leader knows better. The leader knows that the information offered may or may not be totally accurate and, in any event, will change as we gain more information. To teach is to presume that you know. Most of us who have lived a half-century or more are forced to admit that most of what we "knew" we now "know" is false. Leaders, therefore, trust their leadership skills to reveal current, best information available and hope others will follow. Our model of education is far more effective when we view it from the "leader/follower" approach than from the "teacher/student" approach. You cannot teach anyone anything, but you can show others how to learn and lead them in the journey.

I have a friend who stated that he went to a professional school with his mind made up that he would not change it in any way. He claims he succeeded. He knew a friend who decided to believe everything he was taught, and he also succeeded. They both failed. Two sides of blindness.

I have been impressed as of late with the many books that encourage us to return to the "child's mind" and to re-enter the enchanted world of the child. That sounds good. It sounds so appealing, so tender, so gentle, so in contrast to what many see as a harsh adult world. However, the ethic of learning is a massive collection system that keeps everything it has garnered and continues to accumulate and keep everything it encounters. To re-enter the child's world is the antithesis of learning, the opposite of responsibility, the opposite of life in progress. We can, and must, include the world of child enchantment while expanding to a world that the child's mind only imagines and plays/works to create. Thomas Moore states that, "The first step in enchantment, then, is to recover a beginner's mind and a child's wonder, to forget some of the things we have learned and to which we are attached" (*The Re-Enchantment of Everyday Life,* Doubleday, New York, 1940, p. xx). As appealing as this may sound, and as easy as it may seem, it is totally impossible. First, the brain cannot accomplish that act of forgetting, and if it could, the foundation of everything that has been built upon that information would tumble. This would be the antithesis of maturity. The falsehood is in assuming that the world of enchantment, fantasy, and magic only belongs to children and that when we "put away childish things," to quote Saint Paul, we throw away those aspects of thinking and life.

It is interesting that although many people state that God "forgives and forgets," they cannot be correct. An omniscient, omnipotent Being cannot forget and at the same time be all-knowing. Further, the Psalmist reminds us that "He remembers our sins no more." The Scriptures do not say that God *forgets* our sins, but that He *remembers* them. In order to know what to do with what we have done, it cannot be forgotten. We, just as does God, must remember them and as a result know what to do about them. To paraphrase the Psalmist once more, we do not forget where we came from; instead, "we *remember* the pit from whence we were digged." It is in the remembering that we have the ability to change life. Forgetting is like denial, the most devastating and dangerous mechanism of the mind.

6

Person and Relationship

Persons without fulfilling relationships are like trees without leaves or roots.

The ethic of the person and the ethic of relationship are among the most difficult areas to discuss because what constitutes a relationship differs so widely among persons. To be a person is more than to be an individual. An individual is so by virtue of having been born. To be a person is to develop that individual within the context of healthy relationships. Individuation is touted as highly important in psychology, and although that may be true, there is no doubt that all human beings everywhere seem to crave interpersonal connections. The term "cathexis" has been used in psychology to describe the relationship between human beings. This term has been particularly important in describing the relationship between mother and child. The term means more than "connection." "Connection" is likened to plugging an electrical cord into an outlet. In that case, electricity flows *one way*. "Cathexis" assumes a bimodal, bidirectional, mutually beneficial relationship. Healthy relationships are cathetic, not simply connections. To be half of two is to be more than one, if the other half is someone you love. This truth is rediscovered every day by persons who are in happy marital relationships. By the same token, to have half of something may be to have less than nothing. This truth is also rediscovered daily by children who have been placed in the custody of one parent whom the court has chosen. Relationships cannot be parceled out like marbles. It is not possible to "split the marbles" and each parent take half. Half cannot be divided when people are involved. This is particularly true when a marriage breaks up and there are children involved. It is always true, but more so when there are children.

It is possible to get divorced, but it is virtually impossible to get unmarried. Divorce is a legal process, and although marriage is also a legal process, the two involve very different things. It seems that marriage occurs with or without the legal process. Divorce frequently does not occur even with the legal process. There are ties that are not even consciously known to both partners. Some of these ties are emotional, some are interwoven families, and no one can deny the biological marriage that has occurred and can never be erased.

Persons are not simply individuals; they are entities within entities, acting within relationships, and dependent upon both themselves and others. The basis of the person is human dignity. This is easy to say but difficult to accept when put into pragmatic action. For instance, everyone needs everyone. It is not easy to believe or to accept that each of us actually needs every person with whom we have come into contact, including those who were perceived as detrimental and painful. Since all of life is, and can only be, lived within relationship, we relate to both sides of the coin — those who are helpful and those we see as hurtful. What appears to be helpful or hurtful at one point may appear, and in truth be, quite the opposite when looked at retrospectively.

Giving human dignity to everyone is also a very difficult task. This means that we must be willing to believe that everyone does that which he or she believes is the best thing to do at that moment. Even the person who attempts suicide believes that it is the best thing to do at that particular moment. Human dignity requires that we give everyone the right to be right! It also requires that we allow that we need everyone! Our enemies? Those who hate us? Those who cause us nothing but misery? Those who cost us time and money? Yes! We cannot believe in "souls" only for our friends and only for those who do us good. We cannot believe that only those who wish us well are important to us.

Our world is made up of many kinds of souls — as many as there are people, for everyone is different, unique, individual, and important. The role of the negative as well as the role of the positive are both powers. They are energies, and although we may wish only to deal with positive energy, that is not possible. Even the physicists of ancient days knew this truth. They knew that for every action there is a reaction, and for every force there is a counter-force. Without the counter-force, the first force has no meaning or purpose. It is only because there is a counter-force that we require the first force. Without anything for us to "react against," there is nothing to act for. This is a hard truth, and one that causes no small consternation for many folks. They would like to say, "I do not need that person. If I never see that person again it will be too soon." We all must admit to these feelings and statements; however, only in a make-believe world, and a non-productive one at that, would such be possible.

We cannot give meaning to the idea of "soul" without allowing for personal integrity, even when someone's interpretation of integrity differs from ours. We must be willing to allow for the forces of history, genetics, and environment that allowed/molded an individual to become as he or she is to be inviolable. It is extremely difficult to allow this kind of dignity for mass murders, perpetrators of heinous crimes, and the sort; however, they too must at some level have parts of their person that are not always in accord with their actions. Hillman, the noted psychologist, claims that some are acorns simply with bad seed. He gives little if any hope for change in these persons. Although history is replete with affirmations of his belief, there are also many instances of persons changing. The problem in understanding change, however, is that we tend to see positive change as that which enhances or agrees with us and negative change as that which does the opposite. Take, for instance, the conversion of Saint Paul. He had great zeal before his conversion against the Christians. He had great zeal after his conversion against the Jews. The zeal was the same. The power of his convictions was the same. The energy expended to carry out his mission was the same. The direction of his intentions is all that changed. Change may be just that — not what we do but the direction of what we do.

When we transgress one's person, whether our own or someone else's, we force a destructive relationship, and the ethic of our own person suffers. All relationships have a baseline. There is a finely tuned teeter-totter mechanism that operates in all relationships. The homeostasis of the relationship depends not only upon the ethics practiced but also upon the ethic, the core, of the person doing the practicing. The inside ethic of the person may not allow the relationship to flourish as it would and could.

I remember the first car I bought. It was a '34 black, two-door, stick-shift Ford. My dad went with me to get it; after all, I did not have a driver's license and had hardly driven a car at all. However, I simply *had* to drive the car home. My father wanted in the worst way to show me how to work the shifting mechanism, but I could not allow it. I didn't need his help; I knew how to shift — but that was not the issue. Now, after all these years, I see that although I did not need to be taught how to shift the car, I desperately needed to be fathered, and my father needed to teach his son. I wish he were here today so I could tell him how sorry I am for depriving both of us.

The ethic of the person demands that we be human and allow others the same right. Being human is to embrace the continuum from what we call "bad" to that which we call "good." Since none of us knows what is good or bad, one would think this an easy task. However, most of the time we are not able to admit that being good is never perfectly good and that being bad is never perfectly bad.

Some relationships are very short, others are longer, and some even last for a lifetime, although for most of us those are very few, but all last forever. Even the shortest passing relationships affect the matrix of life. They change the waters of life, they circulate the air, they change the architecture of our thinking, and they prove an age-old saying: "No man steps into the same stream twice."

Brief encounters are usually perceived as situations in which we *exchange* but not *change* each other or the nature of the relationship, but, of course, such is not the case at all. Every encounter changes us forever. Maybe in ways infinitesimally small, sometimes in ways very large — but in ways that affect us forever whether we consciously know it or not.

There are many very brief encounters that without question are recognized as changing life forever, such as the criminal who stands before the judge for sentencing or the bride and groom who stand before the minister who asks if they will say "I do." Some encounters are truly dramatic and everyone knows they are life changing; other encounters are sometimes just as important, but less conspicuous. Brief encounters tend to be "forgotten" (of course, we know that the human brain cannot "forget" anything), or they tend to be "dramatic." The encounters in the middle meld into the ongoing experience of life, and some bits and pieces are "remembered" and other bits and pieces are stored in the recesses of our limbic system. Some encounters are dramatic or even cataclysmic and force us to keep them in our conscious mind.

Long-term relationships usually have a chronic, slow, evolving metamorphosis-type effect upon us. We can see the results only in retrospect. We can view some brief relationships and encounters as "flash bulb" experiences and the long-term, slowly evolving ones as the "20/20 hindsight" sort.

Our effect on and our involvement in every encounter is equal, absolute, and 100 percent. Even if we are silent, the silence is profound interaction. Long after, perhaps even years later, we come to recognize the effect of something that at the time appeared to be inconsequential. In fact, the less conscious we are of the relationship, the more profound it is apt to be. Things that happen over which we have no control can often be modified by our intentionality. Frequently we can turn a negative into a positive by our desire to do so. When we do not recognize what is happening, those events are stored in the cellars of our mind and germinate, mold, infect, or otherwise help or hinder the overall process that we call growth.

We tend to think in terms of "who has effect on us" and "upon whom we have effect." Neither is ever the case and both are always the case. Everyone in every relationship, regardless of the length, type, or intensity of the relationship, is always affected and effecting in every instance.

Recognition and intentionality are not necessary for change to take place. It is clear that we do not have to recognize that something is happening for such to be so, and likewise, we do not have to "intend" for anything to happen to make things happen. I am reminded of the young child who, after hitting a playmate, says, "I didn't intend to hurt him." The hurt is still there. The same is true of the child who drops a dish. The child is apt to say, "The dish broke," thus removing himself or herself from the responsibility and placing the action in the domain of the inanimate object, the dish. My eldest daughter once dropped a bottle of milk (of course, one has to be old enough to remember when milk came in glass bottles!) and said, "I squeezed it real hard but the milk broke." Whether there is intentionality or not, the end result is irrefutable.

My daughter's response also reminds me of another very important consideration when dealing with relationships, namely, they should not be "squeezed." The harder she squeezed the wet, slippery bottle, the more it slipped through her fingers. Life is sometimes like sand; the tighter we squeeze it, the less we can keep in our hand.

Relationships must be allowed to grow, develop, sustain, maintain, thrive, or perish. The first few words of the previous sentence are usually accepted without much debate. The last word of that sentence is harshly debated, namely, the idea that some relationships, even marital ones, are going to perish regardless of what we do. Some relationships, marital or otherwise, are doomed from the very beginning and will not endure. As a matter of fact, the more they are "squeezed," the faster they will perish.

After many years of counseling experience with literally hundreds (maybe thousands) of couples, I am personally convinced that some relationships will survive in spite of incredible diversity and others will perish regardless of the heroic attempts to save them. As a matter of fact, I am convinced that there are relationships that should not be saved — even marital ones. This concept flies in the face of many counselors who believe that every marriage can be saved. Some relationships survive for purposes of mutual destruction. Others perish for purposes of mutual preservation. Perhaps this kind of unspoken covenant is acceptable if entered into knowingly by only two persons, but so often there are innocent children brought into the equation, which to me is unacceptable.

There is an incredibly thin line between "therapy" and "manipulation." Quality psychotherapy is priceless. Manipulation is too costly even if there is no fee. The real problem is that most often the therapist is no more aware of whether therapy or manipulation is being done than is the client. Persons doing marriage counseling in particular often feel "successful" if the parties stay together; however, that feeling of success may be utter failure for the two persons in the marital dyad. Sometimes both persons, even when there are children in the equation, are best served when the relationship fails. In a perfect world, such pain might not be acceptable; however, we do not live in such a world.

Persons who disagree with this position may not understand that when two are joined together, the union results in a third entity. Each of the parents may have a fine relationship with their children, but the third entity, the marital dyad, may have a destructive relationship by virtue of its mutually destructive intent. That destructive intent spills over, and the children often do not feel the love of either parent. Sometimes, as unfortunate as it is, each parent's love can only come through when the third entity of the marital dyad is demolished.

There are also relationships that are so devastating that they must be terminated. Some would insist that these relationships are rooted in mental illness. Doubtless many are. However, many are rooted in selfishness, greed, and narcissistic self-indulgence. I have seen such relationships where a child grew up and searched out an estranged parent, often only to bear witness to the destructive nature of the relationship. Sometimes the child had the maturity and mental health to witness the danger in the relationship and go on in life without it. Other times, the unconscious symbiosis was so real that a transfer of affection occurred and the child bonded to a totally devastative relationship with the destructive parent.

In a day when estranged children, adopted children, and kidnapped children are so plentiful, there are many variations of children seeking out a "real" parent or "biological" parent. We tend to hear about those that are rewarding and positive. Professional counselors know that there are just as many, maybe more, that do not turn out happy. We see dramatic, "wonderful" reunions on television. Counselors see many of the other sort in their offices.

Relationships are the most important aspect of the ethic of the person. The "right person" comes along at "the right time" and the confluence of life begins. In high school I met a young lady who would turn my life from personal defeat to personal success, as well as her mother, who believed in me more than my accomplishments at that time in my life would have justified. Five years later that young lady became my wife. In college I met a man who changed my life from academic failure to academic achievement. Although one must be "open" to such changes, the power of the relationship is so profound that at times all it needs is a crack, and like the tree that grows in the tiny crack of a rock until it breaks it in two, the relationship does the same thing. This is not the ethics of persons; it is the ethic of the person and its unstoppable effect upon that which it encounters.

Relationship is the ethic of the experience of life as expressed wholly voluntarily and totally involuntarily by the process of being. Many a patient has had the ethic of his or her being destroyed by inserting the ethics of psychotherapy. Therapists do this by destroying one's ethic and replacing its troublesome parts with a diagnosis. Under the guise of a diagnosis, treatment, and cure, the patient ceases to be a person and becomes a statistic of normality. In this voluntary, yet totally involuntary, relationship, persons change to meet external expectations. Many therapists fail to build a truly therapeutic relationship with their patients due to the sterile approaches and minimal results they have come to expect.

Sometimes the relationship is with a minister, a doctor, a therapist, or even a friend. A formal diagnosis is not necessary and frequently is a hindrance. When the homeostasis of a relationship is upset and one of the parties becomes dependent, the ethic of both parties changes. Although most therapists blame the patient for "becoming dependent," only therapists who encourage dependence and are made to feel indispensable find it to be present. The "ethics" of many professions, certainly those of psychotherapists, have arisen largely out of a response to therapists who do not perceive the boundaries or maintain them with their own internal ethic.

Within formal professional organizations, the interpretation of the code of "ethics" is done to keep the actions of the profession's members pure. The fact, however, is that member of such bodies become self-appointed disciplinarians to protect their view of righteousness. As much has been done by most of these organizations to destroy professional relationships as has ever been protected.

A physician was working nights in a small village hospital when a young mother arrived about to deliver what soon became diagnosed as a "placenta-previa" delivery, a treacherous condition in which the placenta presents before the baby, producing a life-threatening crisis situation. The physician was one of two in the hospital and both were needed in this crisis. The patient was the first physician's daughter. In classes, I have asked aspiring young professionals, "What should he have done?" These bright, brainwashed young professional minds wax into the most ridiculous "ethical" considerations that one can imagine, including believing that the physician should refuse to participate due to "conflict of interest," "dual relationship," etc. I then tell them that the physician was myself, the patient was my daughter, and the baby was my granddaughter — all of whom are alive and well today. Had many of the students' purported "ethical" behavior been followed, the end would undoubtedly have been different, perhaps even tragic.

Although "ethics" are presumably designed to protect both the client and the professional person, they are very artificial. For instance, two of the major ethical premises are "conflict of interest" and "dual relationship." In truth, there is no way to avoid either one. If the professional is receiving compensation from the client, there is an absolute conflict of interest. If the patient gets well and ceases treatment, the professional risks loss of income; hence the conflict is that the patient should get well before another patient is available to pay for that time. Likewise, there is no way to avoid dual relationship. The patient who pays part of the professional's salary is always in the position of both dependent for help and supporter of the professional's income. In other words, the patient who pays directly for services is always both a dependent and a provider. The professional in that situation is also always a dependent and a provider. By the same token, how can the professional not be in conflict with one and at the same time sincerely attempt to help the patient get well yet need him or her to stay sick?

Codes of ethics are intended to define relationships, protect patients/clients, protect the public, and safeguard professions. But every profession changes its code of ethics every few years. Why is that? Is it because that which is ethical changes? No, it is because the "interpretation" of that which is ethical changes. Usually, this is due more to persons than to situations. After all, it is people who write the code; the code does not write itself. People are appointed or elected from a profession to represent and interpret to the profession what the "ethics" are all about. Therefore, the changes in codes of ethics are most often simply new territories of power carved out by new appointees.

Relationships are not created by codes of ethics. They have, however, at times been harmed by them. The human being as a person does not need a code of ethics to establish personal integrity. The superimposed code satisfies society and serves to present an exterior "goodness." This societal cosmetic provides the basis for the public myth of ethical behavior. The judgment is not upon "ethical" behavior, but "conformity" behavior. We know that what is accepted as "ethical" at one point in time is not accepted at another time. That which is ethical did not change, but the code and the interpretation of the code changed, making behavior at one point in time unacceptable and at another time quite commendable.

It is not possible to avoid either conflict of interest or dual relationships, even if that were desirable. To avoid these assumed relational disabilities, one would have to live a most sterile life. To be sure, our society has espoused the necessity for such; however, this was not the case in former societies or even at earlier times in our own history. The early psychoanalysts were known to even go on vacations and "holidays" with their patients — supposedly in order to avoid a disruption of treatment. Ministers, priests, and rabbis socialize with their parishioners, are paid by them, and accept gifts from them. Psychotherapists are paid by their patients, and lawyers are paid by their clients. There is no way to avoid the supposed deleterious results in any relationship in which the provider of the service is dependent upon the recipient of that service for his or her livelihood.

If this is the case, and it is, why did this most artificial system develop? It developed out of the need for power. As human beings, we love to have power over others. The power to control others and to require their accountability to us is a coveted possession among many humans. The more one becomes appointed to power, the more one takes on the behavior and demeanor that he or she assumes that position carries. We have all seen the kind, gentle person promoted to a position of power and change dramatically, almost overnight. Instead of the metamorphosis from a worm into a butterfly, the change was quite the reverse — from a butterfly into a worm! Someone once said, "There is nothing that corrupts like power and nothing that absolutely corrupts more than absolute power."

The emphasis in most codes of ethics is on how a relationship *should not* be developed. The assumption is that what is "good" for an individual is also "right" and that which is "right" is also that which is "needed." In truth, neither may always be the case at the same time or even at different times. To make that assumption requires that we "know" that which is "good" for the other person, that we "know" that which is "right" for others, and that we "know" that which is needed. Talk about omniscience and omnipotence!

There are ways to enhance relationships; however, relationships between human beings are always basically compatible. People naturally tend to like each other. We want to live within relationships. We want to live in harmony. Humans do not by nature enjoy conflict and disharmony unless they suffer from mental illness or severe personality disorders. Most codes of ethics assume the opposite and set forth guidelines to protect us from ourselves, since we are prone to "wrongness." It is interesting that although few codes of behavior would openly admit that they adhere to the conservative Protestant theology of "original sin," they follow it. That doctrine asserts that our basic nature is sinful and that, left to our own behavior, it will always be wrong. It is strange that organizations that so vehemently deny any religious basis are so utterly religious in belief!

There are many ways to destroy relationship; however, human beings naturally like and enjoy each other. It takes thought and considerable work to destroy a relationship. We speak of having to "work at it" to build a relationship. I would assert that although it takes effort to maintain a relationship, most of that energy is spent counteracting attempts to destroy it. If left alone with even a modicum of support, relationships do not fall apart. As with anything else in nature, gentle falling rain, sunshine, and adequate nutrition are about all that is needed for healthy survival and growth. Blistering sun, raging winds, and nutrient-poor soil produce illness and death. Relationships are no different.

Traveling, which has encompassed many hours and days of my life, has taught me that people all over the world are eager to get to know each other. The first question asked upon meeting a stranger is invariably, "Where are you from?" This question is followed quickly by, "What do you do?" Knowing where people are from and what they do establishes rapport. We immediately start to make connections. We ask, "Do you know...?" The conversation will stray many miles and many generations if necessary to make a connection, even to, "My second cousin's aunt went to college where your mother's sister did!"

The story is told of the Egyptian Isis, who searched the world over for her slaughtered brother and husband, Osiris. We will go to no end to make human connections that have meaning. The Greek myth is told of two dogs that were cut in two. When put back together, the wrong ends were attached. Another version is that several dogs went to a party and were required to hang their tails up on hooks as they went in. When they left, they got the wrong tails and have ever since been searching for their own. Hence, dogs to this day go around smelling each other in an attempt to find their correct ancestral body part!

We, although certainly not like dogs, also seem to go through life making deliberate, conscious, and continuous attempts to "connect" to our fellow human being. We feel good when we find out that someone we do not know comes from our hometown, knows one of our family members, or even graduated from the same college.

When I moved from a large metropolitan city to a small Midwestern city, I chose to visit several churches and invited the pastor of one of them to breakfast. In the midst of our discussion it became obvious that our paths had crossed many times without our knowing it. His wife graduated in the same high school class as did I, although we did not know each other. He had been student pastor of a small church where my brother had also been student pastor. He, his wife, my brother and his wife, and my wife and I had all gone to the same college!

The study of genealogy by so many persons attests to one's need for relationship, one's past, and one's roots. Persons who study genealogy travel great distances and spend hours in libraries, cemeteries, and small village churches and courthouses. Some go to the National Archives in Washington, D.C. My wife has a "thing" about visiting cemeteries and reading the tombstone inscriptions. She calls it a study of history! In truth, although I do not enjoy that particular pastime, her interest in it is easy to understand. Our history is our present, and our history is our future. We are only our future as we confirm and identify with our history. There are elements in every person's family history that one might wish to forget; however, growth for the future is not in the forgetting but in the remembering. Just as there is physical DNA that links us genetically to our forebears, there is emotional linkage that is just as strong. Further, since we are all so interrelated, reading the tombstone of someone not known to be at all in our "bloodline" is very much a part of our history and our future. Searching through the annals of genealogy and reading our way through a cemetery are absolute evidence of our need for relationship with the past in order to establish our present.

I wish that I had asked more questions of my grandparents and parents before they died. I can remember family gatherings where the men sat on the front porch and talked about their "roots." They would talk about where they grew up and what they remembered. The women, usually in another part of the house (probably cooking or doing the dishes!), would do the same. We kids, unfortunately, were not encouraged to listen and for the most part we did not. Sometimes we would eavesdrop if it got interesting though. But I did not listen enough or ask enough questions. There are many things that I now need to know that I never will. I was not wise enough to cherish that information when it could have been obtained. Today, there is a wonderful opportunity to videotape interviews with elder family members in order to pass on this kind of vital information at a time when their ancestors will be old enough to appreciate it. The practice is thoughtful recognition of our need for emotional linkage. Further, it may save many hours of trudging through cemeteries for people who find it boring, like me!

Part of our youthful disinterest in our heritage may be the result of the "wasting" of America's elders. It is only as we mature that we recognize that we too shall soon be "wasted" and forgotten. By that I mean that in our Western culture, we do not give sufficient credence to the wisdom and importance of our elder citizens. Finally, when we become one of those elders, we come to wish we had given more respect to those who went before us so that we could do better now in that same period of life. America does not do well with appreciating age, wisdom, and experience. We are a "throwaway" society and often treat elders like any other disposable product. Relationships are not cherished for what they *are* but for what they *do*. When a relationship no longer *does* something for us, it has outlived its purpose. The problem in this with parents and relatives is that sometimes only many years later do we realize that the relationship *continued to do* long after we thought it was done! And by the time we discover that it was continuing to do, we have lost the opportunity to benefit from it. By that time, the other part of the relationship has died, moved to some distant place, or just plain given up.

My only brother, eighteen months my senior, died at the early age of thirty-four of that "life-robber" called cancer. We were both still too young to know what we needed in each other. I clearly remember each of us just getting a grasp on our need for each other when the grim reaper appeared. I am to this day grateful for even the small amount of time we had to at least appreciate what we needed, even though we did not have time to fulfill many of those needs. I am certain that my life is in many ways not only the fulfillment of my own but also an extension of his.

Unfortunately, it is seemingly easy in our modern world to tolerate and even ignore disrupted relationships. Our world is so full of disrupted relationships that it has become a most accepted part of life. Indeed, it is more common to deal with severed marriages, partnerships, etc. than those that endure. Couples that make it together past the seventh year are dwindling in number. Marriages that make it to their twenty-fifth anniversary are greatly celebrated. Those that make it to the fiftieth are a spectacle! My wife and I are among those spectacles.

Since we do not live in a perfect world, and since our choices are not always wise and good, some relationships do not endure. However, we take disruptions entirely too lightly. I am reminded of the many villages on the island of Montserrat in the Caribbean. Some months ago, there was a thriving culture with industry, churches, and a university. Then a volcano erupted, sending its inhabitants scattering to other islands for refuge. I watched from a ship as a subsequent eruption occurred which obliterated even more of that beautiful island. It was interesting to see that very little about that event was in the news. It is as if a culture can be intact today and gone tomorrow and few seem to notice. We have become so accustomed to disrupted relationships that we don't even pay much attention to whole countries that are disrupted and their inhabitants dislocated.

We live in a day when single parenthood, ethnic strife, and international tension are so high, and we are not yet beyond memory of the Holocaust, which our society has decried as deplorable, yet we tolerate and abet repeated tragedies remarkably easily. Relationships are destroyed by many things, even by things that are supposed to build them, things such as money, sex, families, and religion.

Instead of supporting families and the continuity of parent-child relationships, we accuse such relationships of sinister intentions. It is called "nepotism" when family members are employed in the same setting. Technically, the term "nepotism" refers to favors bestowed upon one's family — of which being given a job could be an illustration. I have seen many such illustrations in which nothing but good resulted. Although ugly office romances and angry family squabbles may at times result, nothing destroys the *esprit de corps* of an organization faster than the fear of relationships, good or bad. Have we forgotten all the positive relationships that have been fostered in organizational settings? My wife of fifty years and I have worked together on a daily basis in a professional setting for most of those years and continue to do so today. Mutual respect, the same attribute necessary in any relationship, continues to effect a productive situation. There are many such illustrations all across the world of father-son/daughter, mother-son/daughter, husband-wife, and wife-husband teams that work great. As a matter of fact, the whole idea of nepotism came about as a result of a greedy, capitalistic society in which workers feared that because they were not "relatives," they would be treated unfairly. In the "old world," a business was most often handed down to one's son, and the son was trained and took over for the senior. Many slaves were husband and wife, as well as parent-child. Somehow, what is "good for the goose" is not "good for the gander" when it comes to such issues. Ethicists, or at least those responsible for the interpretation of "ethics," frequently look askance at marital dyads and parent-child working relationships.

These kinds of restrictions are artificial at best, destructive at worst. Certainly the creative, cooperative synergy provided by a good familial relationship is lost to the needy company and/or community. Like most things, because there can be singular abuse, there is plural restriction.

Everyone looks for relationship. The everyday news even enters our world of relationships. We look to see who died, who got married, who was born, who got divorced, and even who went to jail. The larger the town, therefore, the larger the newspaper, the less personal ethic is involved, and the more social and national ethic is printed. Most people live in a very small world; however, the smallest of worlds does not affect the basic ethic of life itself. Life is no less complex; there are only sometimes fewer characters. In some ways, life in a small village or town can be more intense. There is less space between actors and less time between scenes. In a big city, one can avoid another for a long period of time, possibly years. Divorces and conflicts as well as the harmonious relationships are played out on a stage without curtains. In large cities, there are curtains that can be drawn.

All relationships are a mixture of pain and pleasure. Youth tends to see only the need for pleasurable relationships. All of us would like only pleasurable ones. But that is not the stuff life is made of. Roses have thorns, days have both sunshine and rain, and our lives have a mixture of relationships that are both pain and pleasure, often even within the same person. Maturity recognizes that sometimes pleasure first requires pain. In fact, sometimes pain and pleasure are inseparable.

Pain, like pleasure, is not an "all or nothing" proposition. Few things in life are *pure* pain or *pure* pleasure. Joy is mixed with sorrow, and sorrow is mixed with joy. Life is a enmeshment of opposites, and maturity is in understanding and appreciating the contrast. We embrace things that are more pleasure than pain; however, sometimes the most painful becomes the most pleasurable, yet at other times the most pleasurable turns out to be the most painful in the long run.

The contrast in pain and pleasure is never so vivid as when observing patients in a painful terminal illness. The simplicity of pleasure is so graphic when a patient racked with pain thanks you for propping her up with a pillow and utters, "Oh, that feels so good." The intensity of the simplicity is in such stark contrast to the simplicity of the intensity of other experiences. Young lovers are so intense yet so simple in their pleasure. Both pain and pleasure can be intense, yet there is no necessary relationship between them.

Herein lies a deep truth of human relationships. People tend to see partners or friends as primarily persons of pleasure or pain. They exaggerate either the pain or the pleasure and build the entire relationship around that one aspect. When the emphasis shifts from pleasure to pain, even though the circumstances for such are temporary, they recast the relationship in that mold and throw it away.

The "me" generation has more difficulty with relationships than did former generations. Hedonism, narcissism, and selfishness have great difficulty with pain. Pain is one of the primary ingredients of growth, both physically and emotionally. It is not a far stretch to state that short-lived marital relationships may be short-lived in part because these people do not see the value of pain. Even in someone with excruciating pain at the end of life, watching a loved one die is difficult, yet the pain yields to the inevitable and we say, "It was good to see his suffering stop." All painful and all pleasurable situations are studies in contrast, confusion, and a lack of comprehension.

The incomprehensible nature of pain did not begin with Job of the Old Testament, nor did it end there. However, the intricacies of Job and his pain are all inextricably interwoven in relationships. The pain and ultimate pleasure of Job cannot be separated from people — his "friends." The pain and pleasure of friends is nowhere in literature more graphic than in the story of Job. They visited him in his pain to cheer him up. They in truth caused him even greater pain. By our modern-day standards, a belief in God, the presence of friends, and an abundance of material things should have been sufficient safeguards against such horrible pain. He sought a lessening of pain in his relationship with friends and lost. He sought relief in his relationship with God and lost. He even sought relief by scraping the pus from his boils with pieces of broken pottery and lost.

Pleasure comes from within. So does pain. Intentionality is internal. The faith within, the friends within, and the things within are the only safeguards against the external painful world.

7

Children and Childhood

*Children are people with potential –
not potential people.*

Children are people. Real people. Living people. Not children who will grow up to be people. Children people. People with potential. Not potential people. Children. We are all children at one time, and we are always children of somebody. No one wants to be all grown up all the time. This is particularly true if we adopt the erroneous view that to be grown up is to be serious, productive, and responsible. The child within us seeks the moments when we can abandon seriousness, productivity, and yes, even responsibility. Childhood speaks of a period of time during which we are expected to act, think, and relate as children. This period of life must not be minimized because it is the incubator for all the rest of life.

The child's life is mostly not serious, to the child. However, that is only our perception. I have seen children, even very young children, in child psychotherapy and play therapy who look, talk, and behave as if life were indeed incredibly serious. We think of the child as always encompassing our image of a joyful childhood. There is no doubt that many children have anything but a joyful experience.

I have often wondered just exactly what effect unhappiness has upon the rest of one's life. Personally, I resist attending movies that are not humorous. Life is entirely too heavy, violent, and serious to spend precious "free time" watching the burdens and torments of others. I think that the resistance to attending "heavy" movies is the result of my "adult" having to spend so much time in daily life with such heavy matters in clinical practice. I will never know exactly what effect unhappiness in my own childhood plays in this scenario, but probably more than my psychoanalysis revealed or resolved. Therefore, the "child" in me seeks fun to balance it out. I suspect that all of us are to a greater or lesser extent the same in this matter.

There come those times in life when we must let the child out and play in the sunshine without the serious overshadowing of a stern, controlling parent. Children know how to do this. As we "mature," we lose the ability to play, because we become both our own child and our own parent. We have so internalized the expected parent model that we constantly sit in judgment of ourselves. More often than not, we bring a whole host of "parents" to join in that judgment. They come in the form of friends, neighbors, and all sorts of "authority" figures to help squelch the play and judge whether or not we are "doing it right" — whatever "it" may be.

Most of us have many parents throughout our lifetime. We have our biological parents, but all of us recognize that they only did a small part of our parenting. As children, we migrate from one set of "parents" to another throughout adolescence, into adulthood, and even beyond. This is not bad. It is not even negative, and we need not look to change it. The revered elder statesperson is insufficiently identified and cherished in our society. Rather than attempting to "grow up" and not need parents any longer, we need to seriously identify those elder persons who can continue on where our biological parents left off.

Biological parents leave off on some things. They rarely "leave off" completely. By the same token, we leave parents, but never entirely. No child can ever totally separate from the parent. This may well be why adopted children so often inevitably attempt to seek out their biological parents, regardless of how much they love their adoptive parents. Biology is real. It is not imagined; therefore, that part of biology that "seeks its own" is not totally satisfied until it is "connected." The recent generations which have given greater permission, even encouragement, for adopted children to find their biological parent(s) have taught us about the seemingly biological as well as psychological basis for the "emptiness" described by adopted persons. However, we have also learned that frequently once the parent(s) is found and a "connection" is made, the "emptiness" inside is satisfied and the adopted child (or adult) can get on with life without that "hole inside."

It is also of interest to note that most of the time it is not necessary to connect with both biological parents. Usually one parent, particularly the mother, seems to fill the need. However, this is not always the case. I have found when counseling children of divorce that frequently the separated parent must be found regardless of whether it is the mother or father. I have known of instances where a person has gone great distances and to great financial and emotional lengths to locate a "lost" parent. Sometimes a rebonding occurs and sometimes simply knowing that the parent is "there" and is "real" is all that is needed to assuage the deep internal "emptiness."

This is only one reason why it is crucial that when children are separated from parents, whether by divorce, legal custody, or other reasons, great care be given to the feelings of the child. We so often hear, "His father is so bad that it is definitely better that this child should never see him again." This statement is probably never true, even if the only reason that the child should have contact is to find out for himself or herself that the parent is not the role model the child would wish. We fail to recognize that in our minds we see the parent very differently from the view of the child. Courts, child welfare workers, mental health workers, and legal authorities tend to "know" entirely more than they can justify. They also attempt to justify far more than the experience of those who work with children of adoption and divorce demonstrates.

When parents leave, frequently the child, regardless of age, feels orphaned. This feeling has been reported by fully adult persons when a parent dies. There is a deep sense of loss that is not explainable in purely psychological terms. It may be related to the fact that when our parents die, we are likely to be next in line to face our mortality. As long as parents are alive, we can deny our "next in line" position.

The fact of our successorship and inheritance of mortality is often further emphasized by the fact of being left as the eldest in the family. When a male finds himself the last remaining senior male in a family, it can be emotionally traumatic. My own family constellation has placed me in that position. With all senior males on both sides of the family now deceased, as well as the senior male spouses of in-laws, it is not fearsome, but it has certainly been awesome to recognize my responsibilities and the place in the mortality chain I hold.

The child is only the diminutive parent to be, and the parent is only the amplified child. Childhood to adulthood is a continuum and a subtle one at that. I find it interesting, curious, and even at times entertaining to observe children with their parents and compare their behavior. Although the parents' behavior is sometimes more "socially correct" and the child's behavior more "infantile," if one observes closely, the behaviors are frequently basically the same in psychological dynamic.

My eldest daughter brought an important insight to me recently when she read an early draft of this book. She spoke of that period of time in a child's life when the child attempts to mold the parent's life into what the child would envision his or her own adult life as being. This childhood wish includes such things as the way the parent decorates the home, dresses, the kind of music played, and multiple aspects of the parent's life-style. Children think their parents are truly "stupid" and that surely their own future will not be lived that way.

They "know" that they will choose different furniture, listen to different music, dress differently, and that their style of life will be totally unrecognizable from that of their parents. However, then they grow up and somehow take on more characteristics of their parents than they ever dreamed they would. They become parents themselves and somehow it all becomes okay. Of course, then their own children show them that this pattern will occur all over again.

By the same token, parents live their lives "over again" sometimes through their children. This is not all bad. We have heard a great deal about the negative aspects of attempting to mold children in the form of the parent. There certainly are negatives to that, but there are some distinct positives also. Teaching one's children not to make the mistakes that the parent has made cannot be all bad. Parents sometimes attempt to correct the flaws in their own earlier lives by controlling their children. This never works, not because it is simply "bad" but because it is impossible. This reverse process of attempting to control children works no better parent to child than it does child to parent.

The most fearsome part of childhood development is not that which is overtly and consciously taught but that which is covertly and unconsciously taught. Most lessons we learn best we do not know we have learned. Most lessons taught best are likewise ones the teacher did not know had been taught.

I have enjoyed watching "a little fellow" who frequently sits across the aisle from me in church. I have been watching him for a couple of years, and he cannot be over four or five years old now. I have never seen a youngster who is more observant and intent on "drinking in" every detail of what is going on. His eyes follow the movement in the chancel, his body moves with the handbell choir music, and when people are praying he watches to see when their eyes open again. Don't ask me how I know that! I think the older man who holds him on his lap is his grandfather, but I'm not sure. They have many of the same movements, kinds of eye contact, and seriousness. I don't know what the child's father is like, but that generation between the grandfather and the child is surely not much different. The child, the father, and the grandfather are without doubt all, in more ways than we know, both children of and parents to each other! Surely such observations are only affirmations that "the child is the father of the man."

It has been my privilege to minister in churches from time to time that have "children's sermons" as part of their worship services. To watch the eager eyes and to see that every movement is purposeful is a joy. It is wonderful to watch them observe their parents to make sure they are watching. They are so unselfish yet so incredibly self-centered. I can look into their faces and imagine them as adults in much the same way that we can look into adults' faces and see the child.

Children are like the buds on a tree in the spring or the rosebud slowly opening into full bloom. It happens so slowly that we would miss it if it were not that these same youngsters need larger size clothes seemingly every other week!

We speak of "growing up" as human development. And that it is; however, it might be more instructive if we were to think more in terms of child amplification. We would then expect very different things. We could allow the child more responsibility, and we could allow the adult more levity.

Values are simple and pure in children. They ascribe values to objects, and those values are real regardless of the actual value of the object. I remember my youngest child, a boy, who when he was about four years old ascribed monetary value to the metal "slugs" from electrical outlet boxes. He and his little friend, Chicky, decided to walk down a very busy road and "spend" them on a hamburger and a Coke. When the local police came upon these two small boys and asked them to get into the squad car to take them home, they refused, saying that their parents had told them not to get into a car with strangers. The police slowly followed them as they walked home, where there were royally "rewarded" for their behavior. When recalling this incident some thirty-five years later, I learned that they were going to that particular store because "that is where the big guys went." They never got there because the police would not let them cross the intersection of Harlem Avenue and 127th Street in a suburb of Chicago.

We tend to see the child as "helpless" and the adult as "helpful." It all depends on what we mean by "helpless" and "helpful." If we only think in terms of ability to feed oneself or ambulate on one's own, then it is understandable. However, who said that one who cannot feed oneself or ambulate on one's own could not be helpful? We all know of persons, adults as well as children, for whom this is clearly not the case. Children are extremely helpful, even when we see them as "helpless." Children surely need parents, whether they would choose the particular ones they have or not! However, it is not children who choose to be born. Some children are born whose parents do not wish them to be born. However, for the most part, parents need children; hence they are born. Yes, even those who are "unwanted" are at some level of our inner psyche "wanted."

It is particularly interesting to observe how small children have a specific affinity for specific different adults. Somehow a tiny baby who has never before seen a particular person can be almost magnetically drawn to that person. When my second daughter's grandson was less than two years old, I met him for the first time. He nearly leaped into my arms and would not leave. He put up an incredible fight when it came time for me to leave him. It seemed that there was an attraction that was almost magical. When the grandmother of that child was a small girl, she bonded with an elderly woman who was hypnotized by the little girl's "jet black eyes." That lady asked about "that girl with those black eyes" until the day she died. Although all children look for bonding, there is a special attraction between some children and some adults. It is more than normal. Chemical, spiritual, psychological, or whatever, it is not the same between all people.

Watch the face of the contented new mother with her newborn infant and tell me that the infant is "helpless." That child "helps" its mother to a joy that is unsurpassed. That child "helps" its father to a gigantic portion of braggadocio unlike any other known! This is only the more visible "help" the child brings us. The lessons we learn from those tiny moving body parts, the subtle yet completely differentiated cries that only a mother recognizes, and the uninhibited ability of a child to seek and find such primal gratification are such important human lessons that we relearn every time we watch a tiny baby.

It was my duty and privilege to observe and work with very tiny infants and their mothers for two years during my professional training. The lessons learned are far too many to be written about in even a very long book. Pertinent to this discussion, however, is that every infant is incredibly different, yet incredibly the same. Each normal child seeks the same attention, bonding, security, and satisfaction of physical needs. To watch an infant only a few days old "root" to find the mother's nipple is no different than tiny puppies or kittens that do the same thing to find their secure source of food. We do not move very far away from our biological roots. You can stimulate the side of a tiny baby's lips with your finger and the baby will instinctively turn and attempt to suck that finger. Our physical needs are only translated into human characteristics by the emotional, social, and educational forces brought to bear upon them.

Children are immature as such by development and environment, as well as by age, but probably more because of environment than age. Children do not all "grow up" at even close to the same rate. Think of the youngster who in demanding circumstances of violence, trauma, or emergency takes on the thinking and action of adults. We see so often, by the same token, the adult, in circumstances that are emotionally overwhelming, take on the infantilism of a small child. The "child" within us is mobile; it progresses and regresses, it adapts to circumstances and surroundings, it surprises us often with the unexpected, and that "child" is more often than not in physiological disguise as older than its actions. I suspect that when Jesus said "A child shall lead them," the statement was the result of astute observation.

The "child" is also such by "need." Children start out having more needs than wants. The older we become, the more "wants" we have — until possibly we are old enough to realize that "wants" have no lasting value. That age of understanding arrives with great variability in our maturation. Most of us inevitably, however, come to recognize that what we want is not what we need and that all too frequently what we need is not what we want. Children are not able to differentiate need from want. That is because in newborn dependency there is only need. This biological need soon gives way to a combination of physiological need and psychological want. The two issues, need and want, become hopelessly enmeshed, and for some never get separated.

Some persons remain children throughout their lifetime because of deep psychological need. It is frequently a need that they do not even recognize and are unable to accept when professionally identified. These needs are usually deeply rooted inadequacies, either real or imagined, and are displayed in everyday life as serious dependencies.

Other persons remain children due to birth or acquired physical challenges. Sometimes these persons can meet and surmount their challenges with the sheer dint of psychological determination. At other times the physical demands are so consuming that the physical need remains the central focus of life itself.

More often than not, persons who remain children into their adulthood are a combination of deeply seated emotional and perhaps even genetic physical needs. It would be easy to say that anyone who wishes to do so could overcome those needs and move toward maturity; however, many years of working with persons in rehabilitation has shown me that the psychological strength some people develop to overcome their physical challenges is simply beyond my understanding.

We love the child. It is difficult not to love a child. But it is difficult to accept the child who, for whatever reason, fails to grow up. It may be that because our own needs are always sufficiently dependency seeking, those who remain in it are both envied and despised.

Children and adults more often than not act and talk very much alike. If we listen to what they are saying, imagining it all in prepubescent vocabulary voice tone, the discussions are often very much the same. The issues are basically the same. They have to do with things like fairness, winning, whether other people like us, and other issues of status, belonging, and security. The vocabularies may differ, but the dynamics are the same.

There is a healthy side to keeping the child in you for a lifetime. When Jesus said that unless we become as "little children" we cannot enter the kingdom of heaven, He was speaking to a very important aspect of our thinking. Children are trusting, curious, and uninhibited, among other traits. When we lose these attributes, we tend to stop trusting others and believe only in ourselves. We cease to be curious because our egos have become inflated and we think we know so very much. We become inhibited in the name of socially acceptable behavior. These defenses keep us from retaining the part of us that made us human and always in relationship. Let us never allow the child in us to replace the adult. However, let us never allow the adult in us to forget that we are only children attempting to grow up.

As unfortunate as it is that some children never "grow up," there are also many adults who are no longer aware of the healthy child within them. My family plays an annual holiday "game" which would make anyone watching want to call the "men in white coats" to make an emergency call. We shop at a "Dollar Store" for what we call the "Biggest Bang for the Buck." The silliness and revelry that follow that twenty-minute shopping spree cannot be adequately described; therefore I will not try.

Most families have their own unique rituals that keep the children as children, allow the adults to let the child come out, and allow the entire family to be "childish" in mature, healthy ways.

Children are recognized by nearly everyone as being our future and the hope of continuing our civilization. If we were to take this belief seriously, we would take the education, parenting, and religious training of our children far more seriously. Children are the most precious and the most valuable resource we have. It is crucial that they not be viewed as potential people but as people with potential.

8

Parenting and Family

Parenting is a journey
for which there is no road map.

Parenting is a special kind of relationship. All of the artificial ethics of professions go out the window in the parenting model. Dual relationships, conflicts of interest, confidentiality, and much more become moot points.

The most important single ethic of life may be that of parenting. Without procreation and parenting there would be no future for the human race. There is no necessary relationship between parenting and procreation. Many humans procreate without parenting, and many parent without procreating. Procreation and parenting are, however, both natural and unavoidable tasks for humans. Everyone parents someone. Parenting is not the having of children, natural or adopted. Parenting has nothing to do with biological or nonbiological children. Having children is breeding — not parenting. The people of the world are good at breeding — whether by intent or by accident. We pay less attention to human reproduction than we do to the animals we eat. It is parenting that we are much less good at. Someone has rightly said that children are the only things in our society that come without instruction books. It would be nice to say that each set of parents makes up their own rules book. But such is not the case. In truth, each set of parents complicates matters further than their own parents did by combining each of their imitations of their own parents' methods for taking care of children and adding their own inventions.

Humans meet someone and with no plan or forethought produce offspring, usually knowing only after the fact if there is a defective gene that has been coupled with another, producing offspring that cannot or at least should not reproduce. Yet what kind of world would it be if we analyzed our genes prior to duplicating them? Many scientists believe that this kind of human production is in our future.

The ethic of parenting accepts its ungivens. It accepts the incalculable yet very real results of breeding. I have often said that if one wishes to be truly concerned about our future, all one needs to do is go shopping and watch the parent ethic in action with babies in strollers and in parents' arms. Although it is encouraging to see so many parents truly giving love to their offspring, it is frightening to see the hatred being passed on by so many others.

It is wonderful to see so many young parents — both mothers and fathers — bonding with their infants, especially to see fathers who have learned that infant care is not only for mothers. Years ago it seemed that because men could not breast feed, they were not expected to nurture the infant either. This has changed for the better. However, it is also extremely disconcerting to watch as so many parents pay less attention to their children than they do the family pet.

My wife and I were sitting in a restaurant not too long ago when all of a sudden I noticed an infant sitting not more than four feet from us choke and start to turn blue. Knowing what to do, but not thinking that I should interfere with what the parents would surely do, I sat and watched with horror. My wife saw the expression on my face and soon also recognized the problem. However, the parents, with an older woman also at their table, continued to eat and talk without the slightest acknowledgment of the infant's distress. Finally, when I could stand it no more, I went to the table and quickly performed the infant Heimlich maneuver. A huge chunk of meat was expelled by the child, it began to cry, and I sat back down. The parents did not indicate that they had noticed anything happening. Without so much as looking at me, they continued to eat and talk. I left the restaurant not knowing who they were and they did not know who I was. I hesitate to recount this story because it is entirely too unbelievable. However, it is totally true. Maybe I did the youngster a service, but not the parents. They did not seem to care if the child lived or died. Could it be that they resented the life-saving action?

Early in my career I spent most of two years studying and observing tiny infants with their mothers. I was participating in a longitudinal study of the relationships of mothers and infants. I sat behind a one-way mirror most of the time watching a psychiatrist work with mothers and their infants. We started observing the week following discharge from the hospital and followed many of them for two years. I learned many things that we reported in scientific journals; however, many of the things I learned I only came to recognize later in life after years of clinical experience and observing my own three children. The lessons are profound, but in spite of their profundity, most are incredibly simple and obvious. There are far too many to discuss in a book such as this, but I will recount briefly a few of what I consider to be the more important ones.

Many mothers are hopelessly enmeshed with their infants — to the extent that neither of them will ever have a life of their own. These mothers cannot find distance between the nursing nipple and the child. They will pathologically enjoy the succorance of the child and continue it long after the child can fend for itself. They need the child more than the child will ever need them. But in that symbiosis, the child will come to need the mother out of guilt, fear, dependency, and a variety of other needs and will continue to succor the mother even as she has succored them.

Other mothers enjoy moving into the world of succorance, but also bond, feed, nurture, and thrive on seeing the infant gain independence. These mothers have other avenues of self-fulfillment and are able to allow the infant to take its place in the full regimen of life-fulfilling activities and relationships. These infants learn to take and to give. They learn both succorance and nurturance. They can feed and be fed without developing a smothering symbiotic relationship.

There are still other mothers who clearly resent what the child has taken from their body, what the pregnancy has done to their figure, and the crippling effect the infant has had on their freedom. These mothers have a hostility that cannot be masked or hidden. They show it when the infant "gums too hard" at the breast. I have seen them slap the infant for doing so. They are repulsed by the changing of a diaper, push the child away in rage when it spits up sour milk, and I have seen them actually spank a six-week-old child for "wetting" on them! Is it any wonder that these children learn more about hate than love?

There are other mothers who radiate the joy of motherhood. They have a smile that is clearly more than just on their face. It comes from the soul, and you can see the reflection in the infant. They have a tender, sweet, gentle relationship with the infant that you can feel comes from a well so deep that it cannot be fathomed. The child coos more, snuggles more, is obviously more content, and any careful observer can quickly recognize that this is not a mother and a baby but the deepest of human relationships — a mother and a child.

The concept of love is assumed to correct for any genetic or prenatal defects. Yet how many patients I have seen who have not been able to accept the burden of a defective child. It is altogether a common situation for parents with a "defective" child to divorce. The love for each other may have been real as procreative partners, but it was not enduring enough to accept the biological results of that love. I remember so well my dear friends, a physician and his wife, who took great pride in the ethic of parenting their Down's syndrome son. They neither exhibited nor expected notice in how they loved and cared for him. Not all persons are able or willing to be as authentic in their parenting ethic as they. Not all can model Roy Rogers and Dale Evans in their belief that such a child was an *Angel Unaware.*

Ethic is the deep heart of passing on this generation to another. We serve as bridges of the past through the present to the future. The parent stands with one foot in the past and one in the future, and with the left hand reaches for the hand coming into it on the right, to occupy a space that we shall shortly vacate.

That bridge is rooted in discipline. Like any information that is to be passed on from one generation to another, it requires learning at the feet of great teachers. In this case, the teachers are the parents, the learners are the children. Although parents are not the only teachers, they are the primary teachers.

Much attention is given today to the art of non-discipline. I have had the occasion to host a weekly radio program, and if you want to see the telephone board light up like a Christmas tree, just mention discipline. Invariably, the discussion of the callers degenerates to "to spank or not to spank." The concept of making disciples, teaching and modeling, is almost impossible to convey. The concept of punishment as part of discipline is the last of twelve definitions for "discipline" in *Webster's Encyclopedic Unabridged Dictionary,* yet somehow many parents insist on observing punishment as the first definition. Actually, the first and second definitions are to instruct and to train, both of which are more in concert with what we need to be doing.

The whole idea behind "discipline" is to make disciples, followers. Parents so often cannot understand that, and in fact become furious, when a parent hits, he or she is modeling hitting. Physical abuse fosters physical abusers. Teaching is subtle, yet not subtle at all. For instance, it is not uncommon to hear of a mother or father who has been bitten by a child returning the bite, so as to "show that kid how it feels, so they won't do it again." In fact, we don't know that the child learns that lesson at all. Instead, the lesson learned very well may be, "Wow, that really hurts, so that method of self-protection and aggression really works!"

We vicariously give our adult way of thinking to the child. Children cannot, should not, and must not think as adults. Too bad that adults who can, but should not, think so often as children. The child's mind is one that continually tests the environment, like the baby bird on the edge of the perch testing to see if it should risk flying. Adults are the ones who give confidence, serve as examples, and model the behavior that will allow children to "fly." When we as adults are afraid of the perch and act impulsively, non-competently, and model erroneous living skills, the children learn those lessons just as readily as they do any other lesson. Children cannot discern the difference between life skills that will serve them well and the ones that might well put them in prison.

Parenting has taken dramatic turns in our lifetime. The stern parent has been replaced with the companion parent. The disciplining parent is seen as abusive. The expectational parent is seen as "laying a guilt trip on the kid." The sacrificing parent is seen as "doting." Two-parent families are rapidly becoming a thing of the past. The parent who takes pride in a well-behaved child is seen as not allowing enough individual freedom.

The only values that last are given through parenting — parenting from someone. It may well be from others as well as the biological or adoptive parents. I well remember a Boy Scout leader, De Lloyd Keyes, who, when I was out of school winter after winter with pneumonia, came by my house every day with my assignments so that I would not fall too far behind. He was leader of Lincoln Trails Troop 13 and taught us many things that only he as a non-parent could parent. A Sunday school teacher by the name of Lester Wallace, whom I did not know was that interested in me, many years after I was a child in his class drove many miles to hear me preach at a small church where I was pastor. He continued to practice his parenting, although I had never realized he was doing it! Parenting goes far beyond the home. It extends far beyond the reach of genes, last names, and ownership.

Parenting is not always positive — but it is always powerful. The very definition of the follower presumes that the teacher is right and the learner less able to know. As a result, we must be careful what we teach, for even though we think not, much of it will inevitably be learned.

The concept and even the definition of "family" has undergone a dramatic change in the past few years. It has come to mean any two or more persons of any gender, any biological relationship, and legal or otherwise arrangement living in the same or even separate households. The purpose of developing the concept of family was not to give definition to a living arrangement, but to give stability and purpose to the people living within that framework. The concept of family has been changed primarily for economic reasons, not for reasons of greater stability. The new definitions permit inclusion in health insurance and employment benefits and allow for a kind of social acceptance of living arrangements that would otherwise be non-acceptable in our society. The changed definitions allow persons who live in less than valid relationships to masquerade as socially valid and, furthermore, to reap the benefits of the truly valid.

In order for a family to provide what the term implies, there must be some arrangement whereby the benefits of fathering and mothering can be obtained. There is no doubt that there are numerous ways that this has been accomplished successfully. In "single-parent" homes, older siblings, uncles, aunts, and other surrogate have often "filled the bill." However, in our more modern definition of the family, there is often little or no attempt to meet the needs of the family definition; instead, the definition is changed to meet the arrangement wanted by the adults rather than that needed by the adults and children involved.

9

Religion and Spirituality

Religion is awfully simple
or it is simply awful.

The ethic of religion is not the ethics of religion, but the heart and soul of religion itself. The ethic of religion has nothing to do with systems of belief or with theology as a study. The ethic of religion is in the necessity of that which is greater than ourselves. The word religion is derived from the words *re-ligare,* that is, *re* = to do again and *ligare* = to tie or bind; therefore, the word religion means to tie back, to connect, or to put back together. Everyone does, must, and can do no other than to tie back to whatever his or her roots of belief may be. Regardless of how, through education, experience, travel, or mental gymnastics, one tries, we always end up tying ourselves back to what we learned as children at the feet of those who in our innocence "knew" what we should believe. This is why how we handle the fragile and indelibly moldable minds of children is so critical.

All children are taught religion, that is, something to *religare* (tie back to). The question is not if they have anything to tie back to. The question is not whether there is a mooring point. The question is what that mooring point is.

The ethic of religion has to do with destiny and fate, not fatalism or predestination, not even with philosophical or psychological determinism. If any of these were true, religion would be totally superfluous. If everything were cast in stone, it would be only make-believe that one should entertain religion. The ethic of religion is for those who don't know, those who doubt, those who hope, those who fear, those who find ambiguity disconcerting.

Converts are the most intense because they must not risk present moorings; that is, they must have something to hang on to. They cannot *re-ligare* without going back to their first faith. Now some of us would argue that they cannot *re-ligare* except as they connect back to their first faith and add whatever they have since come to believe. The whole idea of being able to reconnect demands a prior system, and we all have a prior system, even if that system was a system of unbelief. To *re-ligare* is to pin the present and the future to one's roots — which raises a question: Can one ever really be a convert? Does one not just add to the roots a few more branches? Saint Paul speaks of "renewing your mind," again the idea of repeating, revisiting, reviewing something that one has known before.

One can talk about brain washing, which is an attempt to destroy one's roots and replace them with new thought. Apart from total destruction of the past, there can be no "new" thinking. Memory as a neuroscience tells us that every single cell in the human body has a permanent memory. If we skin our nose, we do not grow a fingernail on it. We grow exactly the same kind of skin that we lost, even to the pattern of pores and hairiness. The cell develops new skin within the genetic code of the individual's past — for the genetic past is one's genetic present and one's genetic future. Our genetic makeup does not change with time. Only cancer, that invasive malignancy, allows for development of another sort.

In many ways, cell reproduction is illustrative of religion. The human soul yearns for attachment to something greater than oneself. That attachment is the "tying back" to some One greater than oneself — God. Normal production of an authentic relationship with God ties us back to the very nature of a child of God, just as normal reproduction of cells takes that new cell back to its parent cell. By the same token, the person with proper attachments to God produces the righteousness of that relationship. It could well be said that the soul without a relationship with God produces the aberrant, unhealthy results similar to the cancer cell that reproduces in a wild and uncontrollable fashion.

Although this analogy is far from perfect, the primal nature of the relationship between God and humankind is not terribly different. There is a basic, almost biological need in humans of every age for a connection to God. And when I say "almost biological," it may very well be far more than "almost." With all of the "discoveries" of genetic markers for everything from anger to gender choice, there may very well be a genetic demand for religion.

We also *re-ligare* (tie back) to persons — the people in the past who taught us what we know and believe. Herein lies a problem for our youth. Some "politically correct" theology now refers to God as being without gender or ethnicity. Every "truth" that I have ever learned was through a person — someone who had gender and ethnicity. Truth, as a body of knowledge about universal values, is not gender or ethnically related. However, I would argue that there are individual truths that are definitely gender and/or ethnic related.

When I was a youngster, we had huge bonfires at least once a year, usually around Halloween, in someone's backyard. We'd roast marshmallows and hot dogs on long sticks. I remember on one occasion that some "thugs from across the railroad tracks" began throwing bottles and rocks from the alley behind the shed. We could not see them, but we could throw bottles or even hot rocks back at them. The adults around the bonfire would not allow us to do that. Those were people — real people — teaching us truth, in this case the truth that one should not return evil for evil. Of course, I also suspect that they knew a fight would break out that no one wanted and that we certainly could not win.

Then there are individual truths that relate to gender consciousness. It is at this point where single-parent families need to pay attention to having someone of the gender of the missing parent deeply involved with children of that gender. There are truths that are better imbedded in boys by fathers, particularly those related to sex and manhood. There are likewise truths that are gender specific for mothers and daughters; for instance, how to deal with a developing female body is better taught to the pubescent daughter by a female who has experienced it, rather than a male who can only guess at what it is like.

Further, there is gender identity. Even if some individual truths could be equally transmitted from generation to generation by either gender, humans are biologically, sociologically, and psychologically conditioned to relate to their own gender when it comes to role modeling. The concept of God as a neuter gender leaves much to be desired. Trying to teach a child about an abstract being, someone that we cannot see, without a face, and without anything to touch or feel is hard enough. Add to that equation that this mysterious person is neither male nor female and see how much more difficult it is. Or, if we choose to go with the Goddess Diana approach and make God feminine, try teaching this in the face of a two-thousand-year-old tradition of God as a male figure. When we change our cultural moorings to this extent, we mix everything up and must start all over again. We must change every book, newspaper, magazine, schoolroom, college, university, church, and synagogue to reverse their teachings about what is male and what is female. We are not arguing about what *is.* We are discussing what is *believed.* To undertake a reversal of the entire history of the human race is a task that is totally impossible. Furthermore, we learn not by destroying the foundations of our information and knowledge, but by adding to them.

Religion is not different from any other truth when it comes to how we learn best. Sometimes it is not the truths that are being expounded that we learn at the time. Rather, it is the deeper truth that we learn. We learn the foundation that gives relationship to what is being taught. One of our problems in believing in God is that we must spend so much time with people!

Much of what I learned about personal faith came to me in very roundabout ways, just as it does to everyone. One such example is I remember that as a small child I usually became bored during church services. After all, I'm certain the church we attended had no concept of time — at least it seemed that way to me, and I think it also seemed that way to many adults! As long as "the spirit moved," the service continued. To ease my pain (and I think his own), my dad would let me listen to his railroad pocket watch. That watch was doubtless the most prized material possession he owned, and while leaving it on a long gold chain attached to his vest, he let me hold it to my good ear (the other one was deaf) and listen to it tick. That gold Hamilton twenty-one-jewel railroad watch ticked with a definite musical tone, F-sharp, two octaves above middle C. I can still hear it in my head. I remember that it had a front view of a huge locomotive engraved on the back of the case. I sometimes went to the depot with my dad, where he went every so often as required, to have that watch checked by the train-master jeweler for accuracy. Switching tracks, closing gates, changing lights, all to prevent accidents and save lives, depended on that watch being correct to the second. I learned another truth some fifty years later, when a thief stole that watch. I learned that the lessons my father had taught me with that watch were now inside me, and although sentimentally and materialistically I felt great loss, the truths remained.

There are also truths that are deeply tied to ethnicity and geographical locations. I recall hearing folks from the Deep South singing "There ain't no flies on Jesus" at a campground revival meeting. That's a strange and odd concept, to some maybe even sacrilegious. But when I heard the preacher talk about how their ancestors toiled in the hot fields and sweat unbelievably and then found there was no place to bathe, they sat around the campfire and related to a Jesus who offered them a model for hope — then it made sense. There may be flies all over us, but there is hope of a day when we can be like Jesus and have no flies!

Truth is usually taught in real rather than abstract ways. It is often tied to things. Real things. Not concepts. Not images. Things. Things that are part of real life and the things that make life real. Particularly things that are prompted from one's inside needs. I wanted a trumpet very badly when I was about eight years old, but we did not have the money to buy one. I had been taking piano lessons. I went once a week to a government Works Project Administration program. There was a piano there, and a woman taught a group of us what she could. Then during the week we practiced on a cardboard keyboard. If you couldn't hear music in your head, you were in big trouble. It surely was not fun, and besides that, I wanted to play a trumpet.

One day, although I'm not sure just how he found it, my grandfather told me that he had spotted a trumpet in a pawnshop for eight dollars. He told me that he would buy it for me and that I could pay him back by mowing his yard and working in the garden. I don't know how he got the money to pay for it, for he was not wealthy, and I don't think I ever did work enough to fully pay him back. That trumpet was not in great shape and I don't remember what brand it was.

It had dents, a couple of valves stuck pretty badly, the mouthpiece was forever stuck in the lead pipe, and it had no case. But that did not matter. It could produce the scale when I puckered my lips just right and pushed down the correct valves! It wasn't hard learning the correct fingering for the "C" scale because pushing the wrong valves produced the wrong notes. And it was sure more fun playing a real instrument than trying to play a cardboard piano keyboard.

When it came to the truth of "taking care of your things," there was no doubt that I learned that lesson. We did not have a lot, but we learned that we had better take care of what we had. But once again, I learned it via a relationship. This time it was my mother. My used trumpet was not only pretty beaten up, but it also did not have a case. We could not afford to buy a trumpet case, so she made a flannel bag with a zipper on it. I remember proudly carrying that trumpet around in that padded flannel bag. Some of the kids in the school band looked at me kind of funny, but I didn't care. Too bad she didn't patent that idea, since today trumpeters use the popular "gig-bag," which is a minor variation of the one she made for me.

The importance of linking learned truth to relationships cannot be overstated. It is the people in our lives who teach us what we know. It's the relationships with those people that permit us to know what that knowledge means. The people who teach us religious truths may themselves not admit to being religious at all. They of course are.

There are no irreligious persons. There are, however, many persons who do not know what their religion is. Many folks who think that they know what their religion is in fact do not. Religion speaks to that which we worship. *What we say we worship* is frequently not even close to what *we really worship.* When studied carefully and observed closely, we find that even while we are verbally claiming to worship God, we are in truth worshipping materialism.

This is where we must reckon with the similarities and differences between religion and spirituality. There are many spiritual persons who are not at least outwardly religious. The spiritual person often shies away from external manifestations of his or her inner spirituality. True spirituality cannot be displayed, although it can be observed. It cannot brag, although others recognize its presence "in spades."

Our culture has become so confused that we cannot see God's hand in the normal development of everyday life. The struggle to amass material wealth has clouded our vision regarding the true working of religion in our lives. It is not necessary to argue "predestination" or other high-sounding doctrinaire issues. Most of us can look back and see the "hand of God" in many situations, even in minute details.

Either we believe in "happen-chance luck" or we believe that we alone can control our own life happenings, or we believe that a "Higher Power" has something to do with it all. The first, i.e., "happen-chance luck," is the precursor to nihilism: live as best you can and die like a dog! The second is pure egotism, and underneath it all, we all know better! The third is the only plausible approach to our complex life.

Attempting to account for being in the right place at the right time is very difficult. Many persons choose to accept "lady luck," but they are unable to accept or to account for the times when things "go bad." This is where true religion comes into play and other theories get sticky. To say that nothing "bad" happens to us is a bit of a "Pollyanna" philosophy. Of all religions, this is where Christian belief is the most redeeming of all faiths. The Christian really must believe that "all things work together for good for those who love God and are called according to his purpose." This philosophy of Saint Paul, accepted by Christians, separates organized religion from personalized religion.

Most everyone can find multiple times in life when the "right" person was at the "right" place at the "right" time. It is more difficult to accept it when it seems that the "wrong" person was in the "wrong" place at the "wrong" time. There is only one thoroughly acceptable answer to this dilemma, and that is found in the belief that we cannot know that which is in the long run "good," "bad," "right," or "wrong." When we are honest, we find, particularly in retrospect, that things which appeared "bad" at the time were in the long run "good" and vice versa. This does not mean that we cannot know right from wrong. It simply means that what we may believe to be "right" at one time in our lives proves to be incorrect at another time. The "right" thing morally in a given situation may not be the "right" thing in another situation. The person who deeply attempts to always be moral and do the "right" thing has a constant and difficult task.

The reason for this is that we can rarely differentiate our *wants* from our *needs.* Sometimes we want what we need, and sometimes we need what we want. However, most of the time, our wants become so much more important than our needs that we make our wants our needs. Then comes the problem. When we get our needs, we are disappointed, because we wanted our wants!

Religion probably comes the closest to "real" when we are able to distinguish between wants and needs and are willing to trust God that we have received our needs, even when our wants are seemingly neglected. The story of the rich young ruler in the New Testament is a solemn illustration of the difference between wants and needs. When Jesus told the young ruler to sell all his goods (his wants) and give the proceeds to the poor, he had to confront that which he needed as opposed to that which he wanted. He came as close to finding true religion that day as he would ever come.

The rich young ruler was also forced to see the difference between organized religion, which at that time had Pharisees, Saducees, and other less than model persons in it, and personalized religion which would demand internalized belief and faith. Poverty probably does not make religion easier, but it almost certainly makes it easier to differentiate between wants and needs.

Organized religion sets out a creed or series of creeds. These creeds are the framework of belief for all that would ascribe to that particular belief system (denomination or church). The words are spoken and "believed" corporately. There is a difference between corporate belief and personal belief. Corporate belief unites believers in a common statement of purpose and verbalized faith. Corporate belief is important. It unites a group that otherwise would be extremely diverse in belief into one consolidated force for corporate action.

Most persons have tremendous difficulty translating *corporate belief systems,* i.e., creeds and statements of faith, into *personal belief standards.* This is not to say that they do not believe what they are saying. It is to say that these corporate truths are so philosophical, so far removed from daily life, and so ecclesiastically enshrined that it is tough to see how they apply to daily temptation and standards for living. Those who repeat these creeds for the most part do believe them as corporate beliefs. And, for the most part, these same people cannot differentiate these corporate beliefs from their own personal faith.

Personalized belief systems require accompanying standards and demand constant vigilance to translate belief into behavior. This translation can only occur internally by ourselves to ourselves. No one else can do this for us. The Spirit that dwells within us enables this translation word by word, context within context, and relationship to relationship.

Relationships ultimately make the difference between religion and personal belief. Although one cannot deny the importance of one's relationship to God, it is difficult, if not impossible, for most people to relate to God without rich interpersonal relationships as well. When as an adolescent I was making D's and F's in high school, and certainly not giving any thought of going to college, an older couple, Earl and Dorie Muller, made faith, hope, and ultimately success a reality. They gave their time, money, and wisdom to the kids in that church community, and when I sought permission to date a young lady (who five years later became my wife), it was "Uncle Earl" whom I asked. All the religion on earth cannot make faith real as can the understanding of an older, wiser, good role model. Relationships on earth, by Jesus' own words, are necessary in order to relate to God. He said (my translation), if you don't love your brother that's here on earth, how can you possibly love God that you've never seen? Religion, in the final analysis, is the ability to *re-ligare* to relationships that make God in heaven real on earth. We should all be grateful to have such relationships and attempt to be that for those who may have not had such.

In the final analysis, personalized religion is awfully simple because it starts with relationships that are rich in love and hope and continues to produce more relationships of the same kind. For those who have not found love and hope in relationships, religion can be simply awful until, hopefully, someone becomes the first one to show how simple a loving and hopeful relationship can be.

10

Knowledge and Wisdom

"The fear of the Lord is the beginning of wisdom."

Psalms 111:10

Knowledge and wisdom are infinitely different. The accumulation of knowledge is inevitable, regardless of our intelligence. Although we may not know what persons with substandard intelligence learn, they doubtless learn more than we will ever know. They may even possess wisdom. Someone has said that it is possible to be educated beyond one's intelligence, which, simply said, means that it is possible to amass more information than one can wisely use.

We live in a day in which we are told that the body of information doubles every few years. The barrage of information is too much to even conceptualize. The era of the computer has inundated us with more knowledge than we can effectively use, and there is no sign of that torrential flow of information slowing down. One wonders if it is possible for us to have so much information that it could reach the point of diminishing returns. Is it possible for us to have so much informational inventory that we have no place to store it, can no longer keep track of it, that the sheer mass of it paralyzes us?

Knowledge is the accumulation of information. The information may or may not be accurate. Incorrect information leads to faulty knowledge. Whether the knowledge is correct or incorrect is not in itself necessarily a valuable commodity. Correct information, correct knowledge, incorrect information, and/or incorrect knowledge do not necessarily lead to appropriate action. The correctness of information is very difficult to know. What is correct information in one moment may be erroneous in the next. Every adult has lived long enough to see information taught as truth during his or her childhood proven to be absolute error in later life. Even if we act upon the best information available, it may produce disastrous results because it is patently false. And even if that piece of information is correct, it may only work in a limited period of time. The interrelationship of information to produce knowledge and the relationship of that knowledge to available technology allows for both success and failure.

There is, however, a factor in the equation of information, knowledge, and action that is very difficult to define. Some would say it is experience.

Experience is the testing ground for our knowledge. Some persons require limited attempts to discover that a given bit of information does or does not work. Some never make that discovery and keep making the same mistake, never even realizing it to be an error. Others seem to learn on the first try. Therefore, the combination of knowledge and experience does not necessarily make a workable equation.

Some would say that the missing element in the equation is wisdom. But where do we find wisdom? What is wisdom? Most see wisdom as the very best use of information and knowledge. Wisdom is the ruler of the kingdom of knowledge. Just as the king is ruler over the "king-dom," the wise person is ruler of the body of knowledge that we shall call the "wise-dom." But that still does not answer our question as to where one finds wisdom or how one becomes ruler of his or her collection of information and knowledge.

Knowledge and experience certainly seem to go a long way toward appropriate behavior for most people. However, as someone has well said, "There is no fool like an old fool." The more we are fooled, the less likely we seem to be to know that we are being fooled. It seems that knowledge and experience require some other ingredient before we can approach a position called wisdom. Therefore, the equation seems to be: information + accumulation = knowledge + experience + ? = wisdom. What is the missing ingredient? Some might say that it is the result of successes and failures in the application of knowledge to experience. But we all know that even when information and knowledge are applied to experience and it bears successful results, even that same person may not be able to reproduce the same action or result a second time.

My grandfather was a master craftsman with woodworking tools. The real kind, that were made of wood. There were no electric drills, saws, or planers. There were no "power" tools. The "power" was truly "elbow grease." The drill was a wooden "brace and bit" with a hand-filed drill blade. The planer was hand-crafted from hickory wood, and the blades for different molding shapes were hand-filed from tempered steel. My grandfather seemed to me to have the ingredient that put information and experience together. It went like this: "Measure twice, cut once." Then there was the part where human questioning came in and resulted in, "If in doubt, cut long." He always emphasized that it was much easier to cut more off than to try to add some back on that had already been cut off. He understood the relationship between information, knowledge, and experience. He may have been showing me wisdom.

The foolish person is the antithesis of the wise person. It may help us to understand wisdom by attempting to understand foolishness. The fool does learn from mistakes. The fool does not see his or her own folly. The fool does not have insight. The fool cannot gain a following of others less foolish than himself or herself. The fool can lead but does not know to where the path leads. The fool rules a body of disjointed, not integrated, worthless information; therefore, we could say that if the wise person rules a "wise-dom" as in "king-dom," the fool rules a "fool-dom," that is, a collection of foolish information and non-productive knowledge. Experience does not refine that pool of knowledge but usually only adds additional useless information to it.

I read in a novel recently that a fool does not know right from wrong. I don't know whether or not that is true. It seems that it really does not matter since the fool is headed in a direction without insight, forethought, or logic. It is not so much that the fool does not know right *from* wrong but that the fool does not know what *is* right and what *is* wrong; therefore, he or she cannot possibly be expected to know the *difference.* To know the difference between right and wrong, one must be able to understand consequences. The fool has a preconceived notion of consequences that is tied to his or her illogical thinking, and that thinking has no relationship to either right or wrong or any difference between the two.

If one looks at two closely related but widely differing psychological diagnoses, it is easy to see the difference between the fool and the person who can differentiate right from wrong. These diagnoses are the sociopath and the psychopath. The person with a sociopathic personality is frequently spoken of as not being "anybody's fool," meaning that although he or she may be manipulating, conniving, and devious, there is no lack of knowledge as to what is being done and for what purpose. These persons are found in every walk of life: business, religion, education, human services, and anything else you can think of. The true psychopath has many of the same characteristics as the sociopath but has no conscience. The end result is the only value in sight regardless of who or what may have to be destroyed to get there.

The psychopath is the true fool of all persons since right from wrong does not exist. A difference between right and wrong cannot therefore exist. The end result is not "right" or "wrong"; in the fool's mind, the result fulfills the fool's internal need. Hitler may be seen as the prototype of all fools. It is easy to see that the fool is not "dumb" or unintelligent. The fool is not unaware. The fool does not take into account the feelings, needs, wants, or interests of anyone but himself or herself. Jails and prisons are full of psychopaths. One of the greatest challenges of psychological professionals working with that population is to determine if the criminal at the time of the act knew the difference between right and wrong. The McNaughton Rule, as it is known, is the defense for many persons who would have otherwise been held accountable for their actions.

"Innocent by reason of insanity" is, in my opinion, the end result of the true fool, that is, the person who set out for some end result without the slightest consideration of what would happen or who might be hurt in the process. By contrast, we are conned every day by sociopaths who know who, how, and why they are causing hurt but don't care so long as they get what they want.

An extremely important point, however, is that neither the fool nor the wise is without intelligence or mental ability. Therefore, the fool, the wise, the sociopath, and the psychopath are all accountable. Only the person without the mental ability to start down that path could be considered exempt. The psychopath who at the end of his or her destructive journey correctly fits the McNaughton Rule and is declared "innocent by reason of insanity" is not exempt. Because you don't know where you end up does not mean that you did not know where you started! We are all held accountable for where and why we start as well as where and why we end up. The judgment of accountability is most often determined by considering only the specific incident at hand, such as a specific murder or robbery. But this is erroneous thinking.

The real judgment must be on the style of thinking, style of life, and lifelong pattern of behavior that led to that specific act. We must be accountable for how we start as well as how we stop!

Most persons gain a greater accumulation of information, and therefore a larger body of knowledge, by virtue of simply living their years. The elder person usually has a greater body of knowledge, but there is no absolute relationship between the accumulated information or the body of knowledge and wisdom. We speak of children or young people as sometimes being "wise beyond their years." This implies that as we get older, we become wiser. Not so. Some children grow up to lose their common sense and only learn how to behave more foolishly as adults than they did as children. Other persons mature into the embodiment of sage acts and a life based on the integration of information, knowledge, experience, and wisdom.

11

Life and Death

"Neither life nor death...
shall separate me from the love of God..."

Saint Paul

Life and death — two imponderables — are topics we would rather take for granted (life) and ignore (death). However, in order to deal with any other subject discussed in this book, it is essential to look boldly into the face of each of these ends of the human continuum.

Since for most of us life is easier to look at than death, let us start there. In many ways, if we understood death, there would probably be fewer questions about life. However, life is, in and of itself, totally imponderable. We do not know what life is. We are not certain when life begins. We certainly do not know when life ends. If the heart is beating but there is no breathing, is there life? If breathing and heartbeat are being produced by forces outside the human body, is there life in the human body? If there is breathing and heartbeat but no brain waves, is the body alive? At what point does that which we call "life" enter and at what point does it leave the corpus called the human body?

Life and death can be thought of in one of two ways: either as lower forms of life or as the human form. The difference is profound yet simple. In both cases, the egg has life, the sperm has life, and when the two are combined, they form life. No one that I know disagrees with this description of life. The difference is in what we call "spirit" or "soul." We can understand this concept more easily if we put it into an equation where E = egg, S = sperm, and L = life. Hence the equation becomes E + S = L. For lower forms of life, this appears to be adequate for most of us. We step on an ant, and we kill animals to eat. When dealing with human life, there is one more ingredient, and that ingredient is the determining factor. It is called "spirit" or "soul." Then the equation becomes E (egg) + S (sperm) + *S* (soul) = L (life).

Many years ago a movie was produced by the title of *They Kill Horses Don't They?* When a horse is wounded, not even mortally, it is "put down." A broken leg, for instance, many times means the end of even a fine racehorse. Why can we kill horses? Why can we slaughter pigs and cows and chickens for food? It is because we are convinced that they constitute what I will call "simple life," that is, life without a soul. Once we believe differently about an animal, everything changes. In India there are some religious groups that believe differently about cows, and everything for the cow changes.

The difference is not in the life of the egg, the life of the sperm, or for that matter the life of the combination. It is in the added element that is called spirit or soul.

Since we were certainly alive before we were conceived (at least the sperm and egg were) and continue to have life in our corpse (DNA can be reactivated and studied long after death), we are beginning to understand more and more that birth and death are simply two events in the long continuum called life.

The question as to when life enters the body is probably as well answered by most mothers as by any "scientific" measure. Ask any pregnant woman how she felt when her pregnancy was confirmed, and she will tell you that at that moment she realized that she was carrying another "life," even though it would be several weeks before she would feel fetal movement. The moment when the mother feels fetal movement has been called "the quickening," and many, including many in Roman Catholic theology, have always insisted that it is at "the quickening" that life begins. When it is confirmed that cells are growing and multiplying within a mother's body, it seems impossible to deny the presence of life. We have attempted to rationalize the destruction of that life by arguing about when the "life" becomes a "human being." This again seems to be some kind of mental gymnastics since no other cells are like human cells. If the fertilized egg were removed and placed in any other medium to grow, it could (if it were to survive) produce nothing other than human cells. So to ask when it becomes human is to blatantly ignore scientific fact.

However, here is where theology enters in the form of the argument for the spirit. Let's go back to the concept of "the quickening." It was at that point that many believed that the "spirit" entered the fetus and it became a living human being. Arguing for the spirit is a difficult task since the spirit cannot be seen or identified by most of us. The "spirit" is surely somehow connected to the greater spirit of the universe that we call "God."

Arguments regarding the existence of God (or "spirit") have always interested me. I learned of the philosophical and faith issues surrounding the existence of God while studying theology. That is an easier forum for many folks since in that discipline science can largely be ignored. When studying embryology, I learned the scientific facts of how life comes together, but certainly with no attention paid to anything called "spirit." It was all cell biology, with an understanding that everything in the human body is electrical, chemical, or anatomical.

Modern humankind insists on what I call the "assignment of soul." If a pregnant woman wishes to terminate her pregnancy, for purposes of elimination many consider the fetus to be a non-person. However, if that same woman becomes intoxicated and wrecks her automobile, killing the fetus, she can be charged with murder. This is clearly the "assignment of soul" and has little to do with "soul" but more to do with politics, economics, and values.

Yet, this "science" was extremely difficult for me to accept, since my first moorings were in theology. There is no doubt that there is life in the sperm. There is no doubt that there is life in the egg. Therefore it is really quite simple to understand that when the egg and the sperm come together, there is life in the combined cell that results from this union. Once that first cell has come together from two cells, in a process called meiosis, it begins to divide over and over again in a process known as mitosis. Very quickly thereafter, parts of the human embryo begin to appear and the formation of human cells occurs rapidly. This is where the problem lies. When the egg and the sperm unite, is the spirit there? Is it there when the heart is formed and starts to beat? Is it there only when the mother feels movement, i.e., "the quickening"?

In my thinking, this is the single most crucial question if we are to deal with the origins of human life. At whatever point we say that the spirit enters the formation of human cells, it is at that point that we have identified the human being, and to destroy it after that point must be considered murder.

Then, in a further attempt to define human life, we argue as to when "the spirit" enters the body. I have delivered and assisted in delivering many babies, ranging from very premature to overdue. I have never observed a living infant who did not have the spirit of life. Did this "spirit" enter at conception, at six weeks, or at some other magical point?

These artificial and arbitrary demarcations have changed throughout time to meet the growing knowledge of fetal development. We have attempted to time the entry of the spirit by various medical examination points. However, demand for "early abortion" and now "partial birth abortion" makes medical markers such as audible heartbeat and fetal movement felt by the mother of less and less value to medical practitioners. It is difficult to know whether we no longer believe that there is ever an entry of a spirit of life or whether it makes any difference when that entry occurs, or for that matter if there is such a thing as a "spirit" at all.

It would appear that to those who support "partial birth abortion," so long as the infant does not breathe on its own, there has never been a life. This argument is interesting, however, because at the other end of life, doctors hook up patients who can no longer breathe on their own to artificial breathing contraptions and insist that they are still alive!

The moment one decides for oneself when the spirit enters and when it leaves the human corpus, the decision is made regarding both abortion and euthanasia. Before the spirit enters, it may be considered "simple life," and once the spirit leaves, presumably the same thing is true. However, as soon as the spirit enters and until it leaves, it is human life and must be treated as it was made, "in the spirit of God."

When life starts and when it ends are a mystery. If we could determine the exact knowledge to determine these life entry and exit points, we could make life so much easier for ourselves. The wish for answers is not pure. Our wish is based on the assumption that if we could only know the exact moment when life becomes human, it would solve other dilemmas for us. If we could know the exact moment when life ends, it would solve other dilemmas. In many ways, it is only ourselves that we are looking out for. That is not to say that we do not care about the fetus or the dying person. It is to say, however, that we are much more concerned about solving our here and now problems. We tell ourselves that the fetus as yet cannot think and cannot know what is happening, so it is our dilemma that must be solved. We tell ourselves that most dying persons are in some degree of coma and cannot know much of anything; therefore, again, it is our problem that needs to be solved. And both of these arguments are to a very large degree correct.

It is our problem that needs to be solved. The real problem is not the start or the ending of another's life. It is the deep unanswerable questions about our own life that we cannot answer. If we could determine when another's life starts and stops, guess what? We could begin to fathom our own existence and our own mortality. Can you even begin to imagine the changes that would take place in medical services, religion, and legal practices if we ever actually determine when life starts and stops? The medical profession has put an arbitrary definition of death into place. For instance, the brain is considered dead (by most physicians) after three "straight-line" electroencephalograms (EEGs) have been obtained. This means that the EEG is not registering electrical output from the brain. Unfortunately, EEGs only measure a fraction of what the brain actually does and register electrical activity only barely inside the skull even at that. But, on the other hand, the body is not determined to be dead after the heart has stopped beating three times. If CPR works, the body lives. If the body can breathe with forced ventilation, it is not considered dead. Our current answers are arbitrary definitions for practical day-to-day medical practice. They are not real answers — only working hypotheses. They may in truth be far from correct.

Determining where we came from and where we are going is what it is all about. In spite of the lofty scientific jargon used, and the extensive persuasive skills utilized to gain experimental funding, the ultimate question to be answered is always the same. Human cells, sperm, eggs, and life are the guinea pigs of this laboratory debate.

There is no doubt that a great deal of human good results from the quest for answers to our own questions. Stem-cell research, for instance, may provide new organs for persons facing death due to dying organs. DNA research and other genetic studies have already benefited human life tremendously. These research findings also present tremendous questions for the theologian and for the behavioral scientist. For instance, if DNA is cloned, will the clone carry the emotions of the physical parent donor? This depends on how many characteristics that we now call "emotional" are actually genetically borne. If anger is hanging on a chromosome rather than in one's nurture and experience, the simplest clone will carry that anger.

The theologian will have great difficulty if genetic research determines that behaviors that are now called "sin" are actually chromosomal differences. It is now possible to genetically breed animals with specific temperaments. Can we then genetically breed a gentler and kinder human being? Can we outbreed criminality and sociopathic behavior? If so, salvation may be more in breeding sciences than in theological beliefs.

Of course, the results of genetic breeding then raise all sorts of questions regarding human responsibility. Am I responsible for my behavior if it is genetically determined? The biblical understanding would be a definite yes. Some Christian theologians would hold to the concept that "in sin did my mother conceive me," yet we are fully responsible for our actions and the need for salvation. There is no doubt that each of us is more like our parents than we are like our emerging self. Does this mean that if our parents had a given "weakness," we are exempt from responsibility for that "sin proneness" in ourselves? We have all heard someone say, "You know she is a liar just like her mother" or "What else can you expect, he is an alcoholic just like his dad." There is the in-built suggestion that one has a lessened moral responsibility if it is "inherited."

Cloning raises many more questions than it answers. There are, however, wonderful benefits that come from our unquenchable and insatiable search for answers. We are able to extend life for some persons by replacing damaged organs, inhibit diseases for others by learning more about the nature of pathogens, and hopefully make life healthier for all by learning more about the processes of disease and degeneration. However, at the risk of sounding philosophically "existential," I would venture to argue that at the very heart of all of this research we will never find the basic answer we are looking for.

Life with its origins and its endings is what we are attempting to define. That is the question we are trying to answer. We continue to ask the same questions that the sages of all time have asked: Where did I come from, why am I here, and where am I going? We are studying a parenthesis of existence. The parenthesis, maybe it is a hiatus, is that period of time between conception and death that we call life. Most of us are more concerned about where we are going than where we came from or why we are here. That may be unfortunate since why we are here may be far more related to where we will go than to where we came from.

On the other hand, where we came from cannot be forgotten in relationship to why we are here. Our genetic past, our parents' modeling, and the influences of thousands of significant other persons in our life all have a major part to do with at least *how* we are here, if not *why* we are here. And certainly all the myriad factors that influenced their genetic makeup cannot be ignored in thinking about both how and why we are here.

Determining why we are here inevitably causes us to consider where we are going. Contemplating one's own death starts at a very early age. The meaning, or lack thereof, of death is uniquely different not only for every individual but also for each individual, and different for every individual at each stage of life.

To the child, death is frequently perceived as a temporary absence. The child tends to think that the grandparent or puppy that has "died" will be back soon. The adolescent frequently views death as the impossible happening to an invincible ego. In young adulthood, death usually still seems to be something that probably won't occur in the near future. By middle age, when the reality of pension money, senior citizen aging, taking care of one's aging parents, and the threat of dwindling Social Security sets in, death begins to take on a mature reality.

There have been many experiences with death in my life, as there have been in everyone's. They all remain separate, yet blur together to form a pond of questions too deep to fathom and too indefinable to put into literary form. Some of the experiences stand out as ones that singularly declare the difficulties with them all. They started in my childhood.

Children begin to ponder that depth when their first goldfish dies or when their first puppy gets run over by a car. I remember that I had a puppy when I was a small child. My family lived on a very busy street, and the houses were dangerously close to the street after it had been widened, eliminating most of the front yards. Our puppy wandered into the street and was hit by a car. The lady who hit it was very nice as I recall and insisted on getting us another puppy, which she did. But replacing one puppy did not answer any of our questions about where the other one went after we buried it in our backyard.

Do people have any control over the moment they actually die? Apart from suicide, some would say no. However, I would not doubt that each person may have had an experience not totally unlike the one I experienced when my maternal grandmother died. I was attending a meeting in

Boston. My grandmother lived in the Midwest, as did I. She was clearly dying but told the entire family that she had to see all the children before "she could go." She had seen them all except me, since I was out of town. I returned as soon as possible, went into the room in her home, leaned over, and kissed her. She told me good-bye and died!

Completing the task of life is important, and it seems that some are allowed the luxury of doing so. For others, it seems that they are snatched up in the midst of the most productive years of their lives and everyone, including them, is deprived of their presence. Such seemed to be the case with my brother, who was my senior by eighteen months.

My only brother, at the young age of thirty-four, died following brain surgery to remove a malignant tumor. I had, and still have, the same questions and many of the same non-answers. He had been visiting us and "just wasn't the same." His thinking was odd, he was depressed, and he complained of terrible headaches. The surgery that followed a few days later revealed the life robber that would end his blossoming career as a leader in the field of mental health and religion. I had stayed up all night with him following the surgery. Nurses were in short supply, and I monitored his blood pressure and his pulse as it faded while his temperature rose to life-ending heights. When he had taken his last gasping Cheyne–Stokes breath, the nurse unhooked all of the tubes and called the surgeon, who walked into the room nonchalantly, matter-of-factly pronounced him dead, and walked out without saying anything further. I felt certain that death to that doctor was a failure of medical technology. He would try again and hope for better results on someone else. The nurse asked us to leave the room. We did.

It was difficult for everyone who loved my brother, but at differing times and in differing ways. For his widow, it would be difficult for the rest of her life in ways that I will never know. For me, it was difficult, and still is, in a way unique only to a brother. I know that when I arrived at O'Hare Airport I could not remember where I had parked my car, and it took a long time for the security patrol to help me find it. I know that a professor at the University of Chicago, under whom I was studying and who had also taught my brother, teared up when I told her of my brother's death. For his eldest young son, who was old enough to know but not old enough to understand, it would be difficult in a different way still. For my bother's youngest son, who would never remember him, it was difficult in a very different way. But our questions were and continue to be undoubtedly all similar. Why? Where? He had one of the most beautiful Episcopal funeral masses that I have ever attended, and I still remember the songs that we sang and the blank stare on his eldest son's face, a child of only six years. I'm sure that we received the standard and doubtless sincerely believed words of a faithful priest, but I don't remember what they were.

While writing this chapter of this book one Saturday evening, I received a phone call from a chaplain friend of mine at the local hospital; although no relation, the hospital bears the same name as mine, Cox. He said he understood that I was a friend of Norb. Yes, Norb had been my breakfast buddy for many years. He stated that Norb had just died as a result of a ruptured abdominal aortic aneurysm. It is mind-boggling to have breakfast with someone who appears in perfect health and a few hours later to be told that he is dead.

A year earlier, one of my closest friends had been diagnosed with metastatic cancer, multiple sites including the brain. He died in a slow yet fast and painful three months. He smiled up to the very last and had time to tell us many things that he wanted us to know. But his death wasn't any easier to understand.

Several years earlier, a psychiatrist friend, who was as close to me as a brother, was traveling from one hospital to another when he was thrown from his Volkswagen by a huge truck that "t-boned" his Beetle. He never regained consciousness. His lifetime wife read to him and caressed him until he took his last breath some two years later. His death was not understandable either.

I remember an asthmatic child of eight who was brought in by her mother while I was working the emergency room of a hospital. The child was in status asthmaticus. She was wheezing out of control, blue around the lips from hypoxia, and making it worse by crying hysterically. Her mother, who had waited entirely too long to bring her child to the hospital, was also hysterical and fed the child's fear, which was mounting by the second. The child's heartbeat was racing, breathing was rapid but shallow, and she had to be swaddled in a bed sheet in order to stop the bodily thrashing long enough to start an I.V. We all worked diligently with the pediatric pulmonologist who was summoned "stat," but we all helplessly watched in vain as the little girl's EKG settled into a straight line and her heart could not be jump-started. Again, why? So young. What had she done to deserve only eight years of life? That has to be one of the most difficult occasions in my memory.

All of these death experiences, and many others, have many things in common. However, the greatest similarity is found in the unanswered questions.

Life is understandable. It happens and it is here. We can see it. Even if it is deformed, retarded, or whatever, it moves, it responds — it can be dealt with. Death doesn't move. Death is not responsive. Death does not offer a hand, a heart, an eye, an ear, or anything else that we can deal with. We must deal with the emptiness, the aloneness, the absence, the mystery, the myth, the sadness, and the imponderable questions. Life changes. It grows. Things happen. Death remains the same. The image never changes. For some it is the last view of the corpse in the coffin, for some it is the last sight of that hospital bed, for others it is the last time they were together alive.

It is a different thing for each person. Memories recur, even change, and often are not even closely related to the truth. But death cannot be checked against reality, as can life. We see the living again and our memories are corrected. In death there is no correction. The greater problem is that we never get done dealing with the questions. We deny them. We ignore them. We "get used to them." We find religious and other philosophical "answers" to them. But if we are brutally honest, the questions remain. Those questions remain until we face our own demise.

One of the most difficult things about death, unlike the beginning of life, is all the "stuff" that is left behind. Think of the young parents who have prepared the crib, the cradle, the layettes, the baby bottles, the cute little clothes, and painted and decorated the nursery, only for the baby to be stillborn. This grief is magnified by all that "stuff." When an elderly person dies and the spouse must "dispose" of all that "stuff," it is terribly painful. Twenty, thirty, forty, or more years together, sometimes in the same house. Stuff, things with no monetary value but enormous sentimental value. Things that are not worth keeping but cannot be just thrown away. Things that had meaning to the dead and therefore "should" (and sometimes do) have meaning to those still alive. Things that have real monetary value but will be sold at auction for pennies. I guess that we should not become attached to "things," but we do.

The "things" we leave behind frequently become keepsakes. Keepsakes are "things" that belonged to someone we loved and we keep to remember them by. Among the things I have is a monogram ring that was given to my father by his mother on his twenty-first birthday. I have a handmade pencil box made by my grandfather. My sister has a metal cup that belonged to my mother. It collapses so that it can be carried on trips in a purse or lunch pail. Each item has very limited monetary value — but that is not why we keep them. Somehow, the "things" we keep allow us to keep alive some part of those we loved — at least in our memory.

Even in death we do not let those we love go away. We name our children after them, we place markers on their graves, we memorialize them in a wide variety of ways. We "memorialize" them; that is, we do things to keep us from forgetting. The marker on a grave does not memorialize a death, but rather a life. It usually gives the date of birth and the date of death, thus demarcating life, that interval between when we arrived in the flesh and when we left it.

It is interesting, and far beyond the reaches of this book, to contemplate the role that religion and religious persons play in both the beginning and end of life. The beginning seems rather similar except for what it is called. Some religions insist on the ritual being called "dedication" and no water is used. Other religious groups use water and call it "baptism." Some insist on this ritual being carried out on a rather precise day in the child's life. Some religions "baptize" their babies and try not to take them out of the house until that occurs. Some groups "christen" their children. Some insist on specific rituals and timing, while other religious groups are more lenient about when and how it is done. However, by and large, most Protestant, Catholic, and other religious groups have a ritual to welcome the infant into the world.

While all religious groups have rituals for the dead, there is great variation. In the deepest sense, the final ritual demonstrates the underlying theology of the soul. It also manifests the relationship of the dying person to a particular theology. For instance, when a Catholic person is dying, the priest visits and "gives" the Sacrament of the Eucharist (the Lord's Supper) and eventually also "gives" the Last Rites. In the case of the Catholic, it seems to me that the recipient is more passive. In Protestant circles, the minister visits, may offer Communion (the Lord's Supper), and also prays. However, the Roman Catholic tradition seems to place much more emphasis upon the priest "doing something for you" than does the Protestant tradition. Of course, this would follow the theology of each. After all, in Catholicism, the penitent confesses to the priest, who intervenes with God for one's forgiveness. In Protestantism, each is believed to have personal access to God without a third-party intervener.

These differences turn out to be significant in the role of dealing with both life and death. I have observed that it is easier for Roman Catholics to accept help in the hour of sorrow than it is for Protestants, because, in my view, they have been taught to accept another's intervention on their behalf and therefore do not have to "go it alone." Protestants, who have been taught that they are sufficient to do their own bidding, often must first be persuaded that it is okay to accept another's help. Frequently such help is never accepted because to do so is foreign to their theology of individual dependence upon God. When Saint Paul wrote "nothing can separate us from the love of God," did he know something we do not or simply believe something that we have trouble believing? Did he know that we were living with God before we were "alive" and shall be likewise after we are "dead," therefore making an absolute theology possible?

Life and death. They must be connected — one and the same. After all, that which is living dies, decomposes, and becomes the nutrients for that which is born. That which is organic becomes inorganic, and the inorganic gives life to the organic which follows. The cycle of life and death. Which comes first? Which follows? Or is each a part of the other and both working at the same time? Some believe that we begin to die the moment we are born. Do we also then believe that we begin to be born the moment we die?

12

Please and Thank You

*Good manners and prayer
both have something to do with God.*

It may occur to the reader at first glance that this chapter is about manners and etiquette. Such is not the case. This chapter is actually about prayer, but it will take a bit of discussion to get there. The heart and soul of good manners is really prayer.

Our culture has suffered immensely from the loss of manners. When I was a child, it was expected, and actually required, that we say "please" and "thank you." If we sneezed or emitted some other bodily noise, we were expected to say "excuse me." I don't recall ever being given a reason for that expected behavior other than "it's only polite."

Manners are the external recognition of a relationship. We say that manners show "respect." That is true, but respect for what? Respect for the relationship. The relationship may be one of subordinate to superior, or it may be child to parent, salesperson to customer, or child of God to God. Understanding the relationship that calls for simple courtesy is not difficult. To be sure, in today's world we seem to have all but lost most of it, yet from time to time we still hear a "thank you" for the waiter who pours water at the restaurant and other "simple" illustrations of manners.

Although it is most commonplace in today's world not to have good manners, there are many persons who deplore the loss of this human kindness. Why is this expression of humanness missed? It is because we know in our most human of inner persons that what is missing are not the manners but the failure to recognize relationships. We fail to understand all that we need to revere.

We have touted "equality" to the point where we have lost the recognition that while we may all be "equal" as persons, we are certainly not equal in servanthood, knowledge, attitudes, and skills. Equality is a wonderful goal for humankind; however, apart from allowing each other to be equal as persons before God, we shall never see "equality" as understood by most of us. We can say "equal" but "different" and make other attempts to make us "all the same," but we will still remain very different. We revere each other not because we are equal in every way but because we are related through a common parent — God.

It is terribly difficult to believe this in the face of persons like Hitler. But this is where "respect" comes in. We respect evil for its power, not the persons who seem to personify and incarnate it. It is hard to see the importance of evil in our world, and I certainly am not going to attempt to explain it.

Dealing with "equality," however, is very important to manners, prayer, and God. How can that be? It is because unless we love our brother whom we can see, we cannot love God whom we have not seen. This is where the opposite of "good manners" comes in — that which we call "rudeness." Being rude is the opposite of recognizing the value of a relationship. It is devaluing and deprecating another person and shows ill regard for both the relationship and the other person. To be rude is not to disregard the person and relationship. It regards it and destroys it simultaneously. If good manners and the ability to say "please" and "thank you" are related to God's love, which they are, to be rude is related to ignoring God's love for other than oneself.

When we say "please" to someone, known or unknown, it establishes a relationship. When someone provides us with a service, or even a simple recognition, both "please" and "thank you" are in order. We do not always verbally say "please." Simply sitting down at a restaurant table is to request service. Standing at a cash register is asking for recognition. Making an appointment at a doctor's office is asking to be recognized and served.

Many books have been written about prayer. There are thousands of definitions. No one understands prayer simply as an intellectual pursuit. By the same token, emotionality alone does not bring understanding of prayer either. There are many different "kinds" of prayers. We tend to think that a given prayer is for supplication, thanksgiving, help, or some other "special purpose." This is never the case except in our minds. Prayer is always to recognize a mutual relationship and trust that the wisdom of God will somehow find itself worked out in our lives. Whatever prayer is, it is the recognition of a relationship. Just as courtesy recognizes that there is a relationship, so it is with prayer. With all relationships, "please" is the prayer and "thank you" is the praise. Both are prayers. One is for recognition and the other for gratitude.

Ultimately, prayer is good manners and good manners are prayer.

conclusions

Yea and Amen

Whether at a sporting event or a meeting of the solemn assembly, there are always verbalized conclusions of various sorts. At sporting events there are shouts of "yes" or "yea" or "yeah," and all of these words mean the same thing. In the church service one hears "ah-men" or "amen" with varying intonations and pronunciations. The longer the "ah" or the "ah-men," the more pious it may sound, as compared to the elongated "a-a-men" said with a distinct exclamation mark behind it.

The dictionary tells us that the word "amen" may be pronounced with a long or short "a" and literally means "it is so" or "so be it" following a prayer, creed, or other formal statement. The words "yea" and "yeah" mean essentially the same thing and are not much, if any, different from "amen." All of these words mean "yes."

My own spiritual journey has taken me through several denominational persuasions, all of Protestant declaration. By virtue of theological studies, I have, thankfully, been exposed to many persuasions other than Protestant. I have thus been introduced to an incredible variety of pronunciations and meanings of the word "amen." Having witnessed many sporting events, I have likewise witnessed the tremendous variations on the "yea" theme. One could write volumes on the psychological, social, cultural, and theological permutations of both "yea" and "amen." However, unquestionably, the common denominator of both exclamations wherever they are given, and for what they are uttered, is the act of recognition, announcement, and the finality of an action or series of actions.

There are a number of not so subtle differences between "yea" and "amen" in our actual linguistic usage. The "yea" can be heard as a team achieves a score and moves toward victory. The "amen" is more frequently heard at the conclusion of a statement of belief or the supplication or thanksgiving in prayer.

In this context, both would be appropriate responses to the issues advanced in this book. Hopefully, by recognizing the differences and contrasting elements in each of the issues, each of us will be able to see God's "intentionality" for us personally, and thus exclaim "yea!" Then, with firm determination, we can move toward our own goals empowered by God's help to make our personal statements of faith and give thanks with our own unique pronunciation of "amen."

This book is an attempt to bring to our attention only a few of the items in life which we are called to acknowledge the presence of with our "yes!" and to invoke the sanctity of the "amen." It is the hope of this author that such simple dichotomies as are elucidated in this book can help each of us to announce, exclaim, and pronounce a finality of truth that we can follow. I suspect that, much as in sporting events, we must over and over again scream ""yea" and in our spiritual lives over and over again say "amen," and we will need to continuously invoke that great prefix "re." We will need to re-exclaim, re-announce, and re-finalize that which we firmly believe but have a hard time holding on to. Thus our "conclusions" are at best small parts of the greater conclusion to which hopefully the serious thought of our entire life is given.

Just as I have invited you to think about the contrasts in these chapters, I invite you to make the numerous other contrasts that you have doubtless recognized but that I have not included. The power of such distinctions will hopefully help to move each of us on toward our personal "yea" and "amen."

www.ingramcontent.com/pod-product-compliance
Lightning Source LLC
La Vergne TN
LVHW020631100826
845148LV00012B/2141

* 9 7 8 1 6 0 8 9 9 5 6 7 7 *